Alien Spir

By

Ron Halliday

To Yvonne
Best wishes
Ron Halliday

CHAPTER ONE

SCOTTTISH MEDIUMS: A LONG TRADITION

Scotland has produced many fine and famous mediums from the Brahn Seers of the Highlands to today's psychics to be found anywhere from Dumfries to Inverness and beyond. In the nineteenth century Daniel Home who was born in Currie near Edinburgh in 1833, gained a world wide reputation and became the favoured parlour medium for the well-to-do of London circles. He produced two autobiographies and his remarkable gift not only included speaking with the departed, but incidents of levitation. According to Home the spirits of the dead materialised from the 'other side' to lift him into the air. Difficult though it may be to accept that these events actually happened they were witnessed by a succession of educated and well-connected sitters. His most remarkable feat of floating through an eighteen inch gap between sill and window and returning, twenty feet above the ground, was confirmed in writing by several of those present. Naturally, sceptics were unimpressed by these supporting credentials and the poet Robert Browning who detested him wrote a poem under the title, 'Mr Sludge the Medium', a thinly disguised attack on Daniel Home. Such, however, was Home's reputation that when he died in 1886 a statue to him was erected in Edinburgh's Canongate, paid for by his wife.

Whilst Home's statue has disappeared to some unknown location, Helen Duncan from Callander born in 1897 now has a sculpture to honour her. She was the most famous Scottish medium of the time. A controversial figure for some, but heroine to her many admirers, Helen was

1

charged and convicted in 1933, at Edinburgh Sheriff court for falsely claiming (as the authorities saw it) to be able to communicate with the dead and pretending to bring forth ectoplasmic spirit forms. It didn't affect those who believed in her psychic abilities, several of whom testified in her favour at her trial. She enjoyed convinced and determined support which continues to the present day although she died in in 1956.

Helen Duncan was also infamously prosecuted during the second world war for informing a woman attending one of her seances that her son had died aboard *HMS Barham* which had been sunk, but the fate of which had, as was the practice at the time, been kept from the public. How had she found out? Since the powers-that-be did not believe in psychic contact they judged that she must be a spy or gained the information by some devious means. Helen was again taken to court, charged under the 1735 Witchcraft Act for falsely claiming to contact the dead, found guilty and gaoled for nine months. Bizarrely, even when released and after the war's end she was pursued by Britain's security services. A strange state of affairs.

Times have moved on and mediums are no longer liable to be prosecuted for their trade,. But the idea of contacting dead people remains controversial. There are convinced believers and equally convinced and ardently opposed sceptics. If there are spirits living in some other world then it certainly challenges our understanding of the universe as constructed by science though there are plenty of scientists who do not regard their profession as incompatible with religious beliefs. My father was a scientist but interested in psychic phenomena. My grandmother could see and communicate with the spirits of the dead so I had an early introduction to, and interest in, the 'other world' which I've never lost. I've had the opportunity to mix with several mediums on a variety of projects and found the results generally fascinating. A number of Scotland's mediums have published books recounting their experiences including Gordon Smith, 'Darlinda' (nee Rita Breslin) and 'Ruth the Truth' (Ruth Urquhart). They are well worth reading to get a sense of what it is like to be a medium. The mystic Robert Crombie (ROC) straddles several areas of the supernatural and there is a fascinating biography by Gordon Lindsey of this key figure in the establishment of the 'Findhorn Foundation'. Interest in Spiritualism is if anything increasing rather than on the wane as shown, for example, by the recent inauguration of the 'Little Rose Christian Spiritualist Church' by Glasgow medium Gary Gray.

In my view there is nothing like your own personal experience to get a sense of what spirit contact involves though the downside is that this stays as your own impression which others don't share. If you attend a spiritualist gathering and get a message from the dead you'll know what I mean. Some epistles from the 'other side' can often appear on the level of the banal, but may mean a lot to those who receive them. However, I'm hoping to give those interested an opportunity to judge what can take place beyond a communication from the departed. Just how deeply into the 'other' a medium of the right calibre can take you. This is my reason for putting together and publishing the account of my forty-four seances with the Edinburgh medium Ray Tod. During his lifetime Ray did not enjoy the reputation of, for example, Gordon Smith or Ruth Urquhart, but his ability as a medium was nevertheless extraordinary. I think he deserves to be better known because it's my view that he was one of Scotland's most impressive mediums.

CHAPTER TWO

'Do You Want to See an Alien?

It started with a phone call to my house. I had been investigating sightings of UFOs and during February 1995 a number of my reports were featured in the media. As a result I received several calls, covering a range of incidents, but in the main the appearance of strange lights in the sky.

On this night, unfortunately I can't recall the exact date, the voice on the end of the line asked me bluntly, and intriguingly, ' do you want to see an alien?' In most cases I dare say I might have hesitated and wondered whether I was dealing with an eccentric or worse. But something in the man's attitude convinced me otherwise. Curiosity overcame my doubt.

I learned that the caller's name was Ray Tod. He explained that he lived in Edinburgh and that he had been a medium for many years. He claimed that he could make spirit faces appear and that included 'alien' ones: a process known as 'transfiguration'. I had read about it when researching a thesis on the famous nineteenth century Scottish spiritualist Daniel Home, but never seen it, nor ever imagined I would. I wasn't even sure if I believed it was possible. However, after two years of attending seances with Ray as the medium my doubts had dissipated. I travelled on a strange journey, one of enlightenment which certainly changed my view of the universe and our existence as human beings on this planet 'of ours': the Earth.

On reflection I believe it is no exaggeration to describe Ray Tod as one of Scotland's most impressive mediums who deserves to be far better known. In order to give an insight into his talents I have decided to put on public record details of the seances I took part in with Ray during which I witnessed the results of his contact with the spirit world. Several people, having also attended the seances, or having read my reports have described the whole business as 'demonic', 'evil' or just plain 'horrible'. I have to say that I never experienced those feelings. I found it fascinating. But I did debate with myself over many years whether or not to publish the details as I wasn't sure whether they would be believed. To me everything that occurred was real, but those who weren't there might understandably take a sceptical view. Experience of the paranormal can often be a very personal event.

I wasn't, as I mentioned, by any means the only person who experienced Ray's talent as a medium. However, I was, I believe, the only person who went regularly to sit with Ray over a two year period in his Edinburgh flat and who - at Ray's request - documented the events I experienced there. I must also add that Ray read over each 'report' that I wrote and made comments. This brings me to a point that both puzzled and disturbed me. Did Ray truly know who or what he was dealing with? Ray was convinced that he was in control of the situation and as the person who was experiencing the spirit presences - the man who had that strange ability to 'bring through' the spirits - it seems perhaps inappropriate for a spectator to question Ray's view of what was happening. But at times I was convinced that he was unaware as to who - or what - had appeared through him and was surprised when he read my account of what I had seen.

So what had I seen? I have given a report of what occurred at each 'seance' as I wrote it down at the time with some corrections to grammar, spelling, and verb tense or the insertion of the occasional word to clarify events. You will find that an amazing variety of the 'dead' appeared, from people with the look of ancient Greeks to more recent figures and, most startling of all, alien entities. On occasion the image of a still living person appeared - the actor

Richard Todd sticks out, forever associated with the 'Dambuster' film of 1956 where he played the role of Wing Commander Guy Gibson. This confused me and did raise questions in my head of what I was experiencing. After some thought it struck me that this living person had the same surname as Ray and that maybe I was being told something. That the spirit world knew it was dealing with a man called Tod? I couldn't come up with another, or deeper, explanation. Maybe I missed something. Incidentally, Richard Todd died in 2009 in Humby, long after my seances with Ray had concluded.

So who was Ray Tod? Ray lived in a second floor flat at West Montgomery Place which is situated about a ten minute walk from the centre of Edinburgh. The 'seances' in which I took part were held in Ray's living room though Ray was adamant in assuring me that the spirits that appeared could materialise anywhere and that the venue was irrelevant. I didn't have the opportunity to test out this assertion though we did discuss possible venues. I was keen to visit standing stone circles to see what might transpire, but I imagine that what Ray said on this matter was correct. Ray's living room was of a standard size and appearance except for its many stuffed animals - a stoat or weasel I particularly remember - and several artefacts linked to Africa, for example, a shield and spear. These reflected Ray's belief that he had lived a past life in Ancient Egypt. As he pointed out to me on several occasions there is a place called 'Tod' in Egypt.

A brief description of Ray's physical appearance as I knew him may be in order here. He had been born in Edinburgh in 1939, so in his 50s when I first met him, about five feet six inches in height (167 centimetres), well built and with receding ginger coloured hair. He had a round face with a set of intense eyes. He would often stare at me as if trying to read my mind. I was never quite sure if it was done to impress me or a way of focussing his thoughts.

Ray had led a varied life, at least according to the

information he relayed to me. He had spent time as a salesman - selling confectionery and solar panelling were jobs he mentioned. When I met him he was, as a sideline, marketing a hand cream - produced from his own recipe he assured me -which earned good reviews (he showed me one from a magazine) though never seemed to take off. Ray was certainly not prosperous when I encountered him. He didn't have a full-time job and heart problems seemed to limit what work he could do. Many times Ray told me of his time as a singer in a band and liked to claim that in his youth he had been somewhat wild. He would comment favourably or unfavourably on various up-and coming singers. He was a Spiritualist and a member of the Spiritualist Church though I was never quite sure if he was a regular attender and he could be somewhat scathing of the quality of some mediums - justified in my experience of going to spiritualist meetings. I felt it was easy for him to take a lordly view of these psychics. He possessed a quite remarkable gift of which he was never boastful and rather matter- of-fact about.

I didn't take the view that Ray during our meetings was trying to 'hypnotise' me. A colleague who attended one of Ray's seance commented that his experience there, he felt, was similar to that which he'd undergone when he had been hypnotised to stop smoking. Certainly, Ray played soft music, a standard relaxation technique, and we sat quietly for a time, but events could happen within a minute once Ray 'called up' the spirits. I have witnessed individuals being hypnotised for past life regression, but didn't feel it was similar to the manner in which I experienced Ray's seances. However, in all fairness, let's not rule it out.

There was never an identical experience but it makes sense to give an idea of how events generally panned out. On arrival at Ray's flat the man himself was unfailingly welcoming, made me coffee with usually a 'kit-kat' or similar. The spirits had told him that I liked chocolate! We sat in armchairs facing each other a few feet apart. This was close enough to get a clear view of each other's' features. The music would be turned off. I have to say the minute I entered the sitting room I sensed an atmosphere. A kind of agitation if I can put it that way. Wish fulfilment? I have been in many alleged haunted locations but never had the heightened sense that I experienced in Ray's flat. I guess it was a more intense sensitivity to the presence of spirits. The sensation deepened over time. During the later periods I noticed Ray's face altering as soon as I sat down, almost as if it was focusing and refocusing. You felt that at any second if Ray so wished a face from the spirit world would appear.

Ray and I used to sit and talk although he did most of the talking. This as I eventually realised was a mixture of his own views and those expressed through him by the spirits. One remark in particular struck me. I didn't find it particularly reassuring. To quote Ray: 'You think you're investigating us, but who do you think you're kidding. We're investigating you!'. This fed into my suspicions that you simply can't be sure with whom or with what you are dealing.

Anyone who's experience of a 'seance' has come from books or films or television would be pleasantly surprised at what happened with Ray Tod. In the first place the spirits appeared through Ray in conditions of full light, that is with the room lights shining continually. There were no areas of darkness or shadow and Ray was fully illuminated at all times. I can state categorically that I saw faces appear in full bright light. I personally found it a strain to watch his face under normal light and I found a dimmer light preferable. But every time I witnessed the phenomena it was with the lights on and even when dimmed, sitting only a few feet away from Ray, I could see every feature of his face clearly. Every object in the room was also perfectly visible so that even with the light lowered it was more than enough to move about in. I should explain that the room where the seances took place was illuminated by a main light suspended from the ceiling and a side light which was placed either on the table, next to Ray, or the mantelpiece

Ray did not go into any kind of trance and faces would appear even as he chatted to me though the passage of different spirit personalities did distract him at times and he lost the thread of the conversation. Ray did not generally close his eyes or give any indication other than in being in full control of his faculties. I did not get the impression that he had been 'taken over' by the 'dead'. He did not, for example, speak in any kind of affected manner although, as I mentioned, the tone of his speech occasionally changed as if the thoughts of another person were being expressed through him using his voice.

So how did the spirits appear? Ray's features seemed to dissolve and re-form into a distinct and clearly visibly different face - a quite different person, or entity, whatever way one might like to label it. In short, someone else. The space around him appeared to glow white like a protective curtain stretching in an arc from his right shoulder as he faced me to the extreme of vision from my left eye. This glowing wall reached up to a certain height perhaps to the ceiling though I was never certain as it seemed to move as I attempted to focus on it. Faces appeared before the luminescent aura became obvious, but the glow increased with intensity as the minutes passed and more faces appeared. The aura had a strong red tinge at the upper edge although pure white for most of its length and width. I couldn't be sure whether the glowing curtain formed all the way round Ray, but I sometimes saw him, once the phenomena had stopped, moving his hand in front of his face as if brushing something away.

Within that general setting a range of phenomena manifested. On 21st June 1995, for example, memorable faces that appeared included a square-faced, blonde- haired Viking, dressed in simple brown clothes. Everything about him said 'Viking' almost as if he had told you so himself. The next day I remembered that just before leaving for

Ray's I had picked up a book about Viking Scotland which I had obtained through Stirling University library but not yet read. Was this a sign from the 'other world' that it was aware of what I'd be doing? Or was the appearance of this figure simply a projection of my own thoughts?

During that particular seance Ray seemed to glow red, and down his right shoulder a strip of rainbow colours appeared. Ray often raised his hands, palms out, to about shoulder level, and his expression as this occurred became more intense, often staring directly at you. On this occasion, and on several others, I noticed that one hand seemed unusually pinkish but the other dark red. At one point Ray's neck seemed to disappear and his head gave the impression of dissolving into his chest.

Usually at some point Ray would close his eyes and lower his head towards his breast-bone. During these situations he appeared to become a different person physically, broad-faced and broad jowled, altogether more heavily built. Ray was not in a trance at this point as he could still communicate: it was more like being deep in thought. However, the onset of this physical change usually indicated that the spirits had stopped coming through.

As I mentioned, at least one person who experienced Ray's transfiguration described the atmosphere to me as 'evil'. I never sensed that with him though he did, at times, have a less pleasant side to his character which, unfortunately, eventually led to my breaking contact with him. A medium, visiting me from north England, expressed the view that so many spirits could be passing through Ray that over a period of time it would have an effect on both his mind and body. I believe that this could explain what happened to him. The more seances I sat through during that two year period the more strident Ray became even to the extent of threatening me with a spiritual fatwa if I stopped coming along! He also became extremely annoyed with a reporter who had initially discussed his activities with him and then informed him he wouldn't actually

10

appear on the programme being made. Ray threatened retaliation! I don't think he would in reality have done anything - he didn't strike me as that kind of person - but it was an indication I felt that his self control was slipping and not a pleasant way to act. The Ray I first knew would not, I felt, have behaved in this way. I'm not writing this to blacken Ray's character simply to make it clear that I did not view Ray through rose-tinted spectacles and to point out that intense spirit contact of the physical type Ray pursued may have unintended consequences. Ray was unfailingly kind to me of his time and in his actions up to the last couple of months of our meetings when things started to go awry. However, he did change and I've always wondered if indeed the spirits were to blame as the medium suggested.

One of the particularly fascinating aspects of seances with Ray was the appearance of alien faces - aliens must have souls too was Ray's attitude. It was, of course, what had attracted me to go there in the first place. But the 'aliens' were only one segment of a panorama of spirits who 'came through'.

So, to go back to a key question which continually puzzled me, was Ray fully aware of what was happening? I've noted that I came to realise that Ray only became cognisant of what had transpired during the seances when he read my account of events. Even more curious - or worrying - comes from the comments relayed to me by another witness. According to his report, he questioned the spirits about Ray and got the response (via Ray presumably) who's Ray?' Odd, if accurate. I never attempted to communicate with those that came through - I was quite content to observe, apprehensive, partly, on Ray's advice, that contact with the spirit world would probably be broken if I attempted to go beyond observing. Furthermore, I admit I sometimes felt nervous about crossing the boundary of spectating and entering a deeper relationship with the unknown.

What was Ray's philosophy? From the list he gave me

(see appendix I) it was nothing sophisticated or enlightening. Ray had no special philosophical insights. I would have to say that I felt that I was better versed in history and the nature of religion than Ray who often made statements on these subjects which I mentally questioned and disagreed with, but I never voiced my doubts. Why? Partly I did not want to upset him or disturb his equilibrium, but mainly because Ray was a medium of huge ability and knew more of the spirit world than I could claim to. However, there was little to be learned from Ray's philosophy and I doubt if Ray would have taken on board any contradictions or arguments from me in any case. It would just have riled him! He knew the spirits - I didn't! That would have been his response.

Finally, it was thanks to Ray that I wrote an account of each seance. 'Otherwise you'll forget', he said. He was so, so right. Looking back I guess he sensed that eventually I would do something useful with them.

According to a note I have Ray appears to have told me that he began transfiguring in 1986. How that came about I did not, unfortunately, ask him. Was it a sudden revelation? A gradual awareness? It would be interesting to know. I went out twice with Ray. I took him to the Aberdeenshire village of Johnshaven to visit a house which had been plagued by poltergeist activity. According to Ray, the occupant had drawn unwanted spirits by making use of a ouija board. He seemed to calm the spirits down - at least for a time. Further details can be found in my book, 'Evil Scotland'. We also visited Rosslyn Chapel. My memory of this trip is fixed on one incident during which Ray simply by placing his hands around the rods I was using to dowse managed to get them to move first one way and then another. I was amazed. Telekinesis before your very eyes!

One final issue crops up in my mind from time to time. If the faces that appeared were not of the departed were they meant to convey an idea, or point you in a direction of thought? Since 'Zeus' did not exist why did the face of this

Greek god appear to me? A quarter of a century on I have to confess that I still have not come to any definite conclusion.

CHAPTER THREE

The Seances

The following are accounts of my experiences as a 'sitter' in a series of seances with Ray Tod. I can state categorically that what took place were the events I witnessed.

SEANCE SUNDAY 19th MARCH 1995*
When I first went to Ray's house, I wasn't sure what to expect. I'd read about transfiguration and although I'd met and seen many mediums in action I just wasn't sure how this would work through Ray in practice.

I chatted to Ray for quite a while before he began to demonstrate his mediumship. I think things started happening around 9.30pm. I could quite definitely see his face changing as I watched. The first face I saw looked very much like my father's although he is alive. I don't know whether this was intended as a symbolic message. (I've had further thoughts on this - see below). Several faces appeared after that although now I can't remember them distinctly except a thin-faced bald-headed man, very severe looking, not a person to trifle with I would guess. There was also a person with a monocle followed by an Egyptian-looking type. Ray mentioned to me an 'alien' face and at one point it seemed as if that was about to emerge: I glimpsed it for a second, but it didn't stay.

All the while there was a kind of shimmering effect around Ray with a reddish glow. At times Ray appeared almost translucent and I felt that I was looking through him. (I have remembered that my father is also the double of Frederic Myers, founder in the nineteenth century of the Society for Psychical Research.)

* * *

On the occasion of my second visit the effect was much stronger although I hadn't expected it. I did think it might be weaker because [name omitted] wasn't present as I had the feeling that she was helping to create the atmosphere which made it easier for Ray to work. However, by the end of our meeting I had no doubt that the effect was getting stronger and stronger. The number of faces that materialised was less than on our first meeting, but much firmer in appearance and well formed. Not only the faces were visible, but also the upper part of the body. The thin-faced, severe, bald-headed gentleman appeared. As did the man with the monocle. One of the best, that is strongest faces, I thought I recognised as Cavour, the nineteenth century Italian nationalist. I had seen an identical photograph, I was sure. However, when I was looking through some magazines a few days later I caught sight of a photo of Charles Fort - the investigator in the early twentieth century of anomalous phenomena - and recognised him as the figure I'd seen.

During the appearance of the faces the effect around Ray was remarkable and growing stronger. The whole room seemed to glow bright red and close in around us. The faces that appeared seemed to become more intimate as if welcoming us into a gathering. I would add a few comments: (i) I said to Ray at one point that women did not seem to appear: shortly after a female looking face materialised (ii) the spirits do not try to talk or communicate or, for example, smile (iii) the faces appear in front of Ray's face, almost over it.

*This was my first surviving report. I must have attended an earlier seance but it appears to have been incorporated with that of 19th March.

SEANCE TUESDAY 21st MARCH 1995
Again, we started the evening by spending quite some time chatting. During this period I had the distinct impression that faces were forming. Eventually, Ray went

into a trance.

The first face that appeared was a surly looking person I had seen before. Then came the monocled person who Ray later told me was the 'doorkeeper'. Faces then emerged thick and fast: the bald-headed gentleman - quite severe and haughty looking. I'm sure I caught sight of my grandfather [my father's father]. There was a man with fair, short cut frizzy hair. These figures all looked normal.

However, three (or two) alien faces appeared. One had a face which was a cross between a dog and a lion except that it had no hair. It was very grey and puffy looking, but there was clearly an intelligence behind it. Then there came over the 'Communion' type alien*: grey coloured with a greenish tinge. The eyes, however, were unlike the picture on the cover of Whitley Strieber's book being a normal round shape, but with thick over-folds of skin which made them look a bit like a chameleon's in appearance. When the eyelids (or skin coverings) came together the eyes disappeared beneath the skin. This was one of the few times I saw facial movement on the faces that appeared. It was either this face or another very like it that materialised later. It was more real looking than the earlier one, perhaps being more solidly formed. It was a sort of deathly grey white in colour, fleshier than the earlier face which had a tauter appearance as if the skin was drawn tightly over the bones. It was distinctly alien, reminiscent of an escapee from 'Star Wars'. On no occasion did the faces overtly attempt to communicate with me.

As I left Ray's I was pondering over the issue of how Ray could control unwelcome 'visitors'. As I crossed the street to get to my car I saw a sign at the P.O. sorting office which read, 'All visitors must report to the doorkeeper'! It was exactly as Ray had told me that the 'visitors' were controlled. I felt this was more than simple coincidence.

*'Communion' by USA author Whitley Strieber, published in 1987 was a hugely popular book at the time which depicted on its' cover an alien figure the author

claimed to have encountered. The image became the stereotype for an alien entity for a period and still influences depictions up to the present day.

SEANCE WEDNESDAY 12th APRIL 1995

This meeting with Ray was notable for three things. First, most of the faces which I had seen on earlier occasions did not appear. Second, Ray's 'gatekeeper' was in constant attendance, and appeared especially watchful. Third, ... I'll come to that later!

I could sense the atmosphere as soon as I entered Ray's sitting room. It just seemed to envelop you although I felt less sure than previously that the faces would appear. The first face I saw (after the gatekeeper's) was the double of Peter Sellers with greying, short hair: typical expression on his face. I was dumbstruck! Even more surprising when I got home there was a film with Peter Sellers in it on TV! And his character made a remark about the 'doorkeeper'.

A spirit entity appeared with a bald domed forehead and glasses: another with a centre parting and medium length straight black hair, but hanging down on one side. A third materialised having a bald head, pallid face with lines over the lower part of the face. It looked semi-human. One face had the appearance of a 1960s hippy type - long hair, beard, round glasses - a bit like John Lennon, but not as definite as the Peter Sellers face.

Towards the end there was a very tense scene for me - it was almost as if Ray had disappeared. Then a spirit materialised with its upper body, very pale, almost chalky white. Then 'it' appeared. An unmistakable alien face. There was no warning, it was just suddenly there. Very clear. It had a small head with large blank eyes. The head was not identical to the 'Communion' drawing being much rounder in shape. It was a kind of silvery coloured head. The head was low down on shiny material which looked like the upper part of a space suit. I should add that the head was bald. The face was looking straight at me. I sensed it was

17

challenging: not in a threatening way, but as if to say, 'here I am what do you intend doing?' (Ray later confirmed that the alien had simply barged in.)

I certainly got the impression of power. It seemed to me that not even Ray's 'doorkeeper' could have kept it out. I was certainly willing the alien to appear as, I think, was Ray. Its' attitude struck me as being different from other faces. During this time I noticed a dark area, bluish or purple black, around the centre of Ray's body. As usual the area around us seemed to be glowing red and distorted as if disintegrating.

SEANCE WEDNESDAY 19th APRIL 1995

Because of various factors I wasn't feeling as relaxed as at the previous meeting so I wondered if I would have the same experiences. It didn't seem to make any difference although I did notice that the shimmering effect I'd seen before was not as pronounced and seemed to be concentrated around Ray.

A mixture of folk 'came through', but not as many as on the last occasion. They looked like figures from the nineteenth century. There were several interesting aspects:

(i) the spirit with the completely bald head, very lined face, almost parchment-like skin was present for what seemed like long stretches - his head didn't strike me as having been deliberately shaved, skin-head style, but it was as if he had been born that way. I felt a bit uncomfortable almost as if he was trying to judge if I was really interested in seeing more.

(ii) at one point Ray's face became almost walnut like in colour and appeared to broaden out across the jaw - at the same time his hands were glowing pink. His clothes seemed to turn brown. With this spirit I had the distinct impression of clothes of a bright colour.

(iii) Ray demonstrated to me that he could chat and allow faces to appear almost at will. At one point it seemed as if another person was speaking through Ray, talking of priests having been determined to crush 'people like me' and saying,' this is the way it used to be done.'

(iv) at another point, Ray seemed to shrink and almost vanished. His head also appeared to compress and looked like a squashed ball with big lips.

SEANCE MONDAY Ist MAY 1995

Ray asked me to sum up my impressions of him and his mediumship.

To go back to the beginning, when Ray first got in touch with me I was intrigued, but needed to see the evidence to be convinced. I brought a colleague along, but he didn't want to look! So at our first meeting it was left to me. I was astonished by what I saw and what I've seen since. Whatever the source of the phenomena, something strange is certainly taking place. Some people would - and have - made the suggestion that hypnotism is the explanation. But in that case it would have to be self induced which I don't believe to be what is happening. And even if the spirits that materialised were projections of my own mind why would it be these particular ones that appear? Most of the faces mean nothing to me and the one I originally came to see - the alien - has manifested only occasionally although with enough drama to convince me that its' appearance isn't just the product of wishful thinking on my part.

Although Ray might disagree, I feel that there is a two way relationship at work between Ray and whoever is involved with him at a particular point. Ray is clearly the key, but the observer is somehow interacting with him to materialise these spirits. Or, to put it another way, Ray might argue that as the faces are appearing through him they would appear even if no one was looking, for example, as a film reel would show pictures even if no audience was present. I don't think it works like that in this case and that somehow Ray's ability is linking with whatever psychic awareness an observer might possess to materialise the spirits.

19

Strange though it may seem, I have never experienced as an adult anything which I can't explain - until I met Ray.* What is noticeable is that Ray is very down- to-earth both in his life and in relation to his ability. Even though he is by nature a businessman he makes no effort to gain from this remarkable talent of his. I don't just mean financially, but in terms of having something to tell the world. Ray has definite ideas about who is coming through and how his mediumship relates to religion and even politics. As an observer, I'm inclined to be more wary. As I wrote of the 12th April meeting, the alien simply walked in exuding authority. I get no sense of evil from these faces, let me say right away. There's an eagerness, curiosity, arrogance, and amusement plus a bit of watchfulness, but I feel an air of protection rather than threat.

Ray strikes me as being defiantly ordinary. Almost as if he is working hard to counteract his amazing ability. Ray assures me he is in complete control of the phenomena, but would that always be the case? Under every circumstance? Watching Ray it sometimes feels like looking into another dimension through a peephole. How far can you really see? I have no answer to it, but I suspect that Ray knows a good deal more than he is prepared to say.+

*On reflection this may be an exaggeration!

+Having mulled this over for years I'm less sure of that now than I was at the time.

SEANCE WEDNESDAY 3rd MAY 1995

On this occasion a large number of spirits appeared. The most notable was that of Peter Cook (the television comedian). When his face materialised the first time I could hardly believe my eyes. I thought I must be imagining it. Then it appeared a second time and there was no doubt who it was. It was definitely the face of Peter Cook. The face was young looking (no lines or wrinkles) though the hair was definitely greyish. He was there for what seemed ages as if to confirm, 'yes, it is me.'

A face which stood out displayed very prominent eyes (dark) and also dark bushy hair. It seemed to come right up to me, something I hadn't experienced previously. One other thing: I'm sure this particular person was looking at me side on. Every other face has been looking directly at me. A man with glasses, bald on top, hair down the sides appeared frequently. I also saw one of the spirits I had been accustomed to seeing: a man with a shiny bald head, high forehead, pale almost yellowish skin. He has an alien look about him and appears at every meeting.

On a general point, I noticed that the shimmering effect was less and all the activity seemed concentrated around Ray's chair. Just before Ray's contact appeared, I felt a bit queasy in the stomach area and Ray explained that this was a sign of the presence of spirits with me.

SEANCE WEDNESDAY 17th MAY 1995

The following is a list of the spirit faces that appeared during my meeting with Ray:

1. A bald-headed man, long face with only a line of hair running down the middle of his head.

2. Eric Porter - the actor, probably best remembered for his role in the 'Forsyte Saga' television series - who had died only a couple of days earlier. It was one of those occasions when you can hardly believe your own eyes.

3. Next a face that looked as if it came from the eighteenth century with hair parted in the centre and the rest curled down the sides of the head.

4. The bald-headed person with the deeply lined face appeared again (as he always does).

5. One face appeared, almost round like a squashed up tennis ball.

6. Peter Sellers appeared again, displaying a vivid face but with yellowish hair.

7. A man who looked as if he came from the nineteenth century with a bald head and long hair down the sides and wearing round glasses. (I have seen him several times

before.)

8. A young-looking face, hippy type, with bushy hair and round glasses (I have seen him before).

The faces that materialised later looked solid like marble or painted.

At one point, after I'd seen Eric Porter, Ray suddenly started talking in a strange language as he slumped back as if in a trance with eyes closed, looking like a statue of the Buddha with its' swollen stomach. After this incident there was a flood of faces, too many in fact to remember. Ray informed me that the faces would appear whether another person was there or not.* He also informed me that he had seen someone sitting with me. I had felt queasy at this point.

*I don't think Ray meant he could see these faces as I'm sure he couldn't but he could, of course, sense and feel their presence. Had he ever looked in a mirror? I don't honestly remember if I ever asked him this. If he had would he have seen them? It's an interesting question.

SEANCE WEDNESDAY 24th MAY 1995

The faces I witnessed were as follows:

(1) A puffy faced alien. The face was light grey, round shaped with what seemed like tubes running from the back of the head in a circular shape to the back of the neck. The most striking aspect, however, was the eyes which were prominent, but with no proper eyeballs in the sense that we would recognise. I did get the feeling, however, that he (or she?) was staring at me. The head was completely bald, or, at least, looked extremely smooth. At this point Ray had his eyes closed. The face was very lined.

(2) A person I have often seen with black hair and round glasses.

At this point Ray informed me that I would see someone I would recognise and faces started to appear thick and fast.

(3) There was a lady with black, curly hair, but in a style with the hair made up on the top of her head. This person was sideways or at an angle rather than face on, the position

in which most appear.

(4) Before the above I recall that a very long faced, sandy complexioned individual appeared.

The power was certainly building up, but at this juncture the phone went which caused me to about jump out of my seat. Fortunately, Ray managed to keep calm.

(5) On resuming, the most memorable face I saw was that of Richard Todd, or someone who looked very much like him. He was a well known actor from the 1950s best remembered for his role in the 'Dambusters' film and playing 'Robin Hood' among many other acting parts. Now here is the odd aspect. Ray had been thinking about Clark Gable who does indeed look like Tod, particularly the hairstyle. Why should Tod appear and not Gable? Is there a link which we could find - I am certainly looking into this*. Why, I wonder, have so many famous actors appeared to us?

   * I don't think I did!

SEANCE MONDAY 29th MAY 1995

On this occasion I was not sitting directly opposite but was situated slightly at an angle so I could see Ray from the side. A colleague was with me and on a number of occasions it was clear that we were seeing the same faces although I saw some that my colleague didn't see and vice versa.

These were the faces that I remember:

1) A face with a big beard and glasses. My colleague likened the person to Rolf Harris although it struck me as having a nineteenth century look.

2) Most remarkably I saw Winston Churchill, twice as a young man and then when he was older. He was looking very cheerful. Ray informed me later that a programme, 'The Churchills', had been on TV earlier that week and it crossed his mind that it would be nice if he would give us a visit! I wasn't thinking about Churchill at the time or within the few days previously. It was a very clear sight and as

before when I've seen a well known person I can hardly believe my eyes.

3) A face which looked as if it was stretched back like flattened marble.

4) I saw numerous grey faces and at one point I could see ectoplasm - it looked as if a coat of white was stretching out of Ray's face.

5) At one point it looked as if Ray was covered by a kind of red blanket.

6)   I saw the bald headed man with the ridge going from the front to the back of his head and with a very straight nose. My colleague confirmed this sighting.

SEANCE WEDNESDAY 7th JUNE 1995

The spirits that materialised were as follows:

1. An individual who looked like me and kept appearing. As he materialised Ray continued to talk and thus was completely awake and aware as this was happening. I should add that, being the month of June, it was bright daylight at this time. The 'face' had a beard with curly hair which seemed to stand up. The person reappeared later, looking older. It was as if it was saying 'do you recognise me now?' I felt that I should be able to recognise him, but unfortunately couldn't.

2. An alien appeared with bony bits around the side of its' head.

3. A person with an oval shaped face, thinning black hair well back from a high forehead. He looked like a teacher I met at Fortrose Academy in 1972 on the 'Black Isle' when I was doing teacher training there.

4. 'It' looked like a gorilla - just flashed by - although the hair seemed brownish rather than black. It might have been a very hairy man like the film portrayal of a werewolf. Or was the message that man and gorillas are not far apart?

5. Many elderly, greying faces passed by.

6. The bald-headed person with the lined face appeared.

7. A woman with very white hair in a bouffant style. Looked middle-aged and peaceful. This face was more side-on than straight on. It was a broad face, friendly.

At one point Ray's whole body seemed to glow. I can confirm that Ray seems able to allow the spirits to appear at will.

SEANCE WEDNESDAY 26th JULY 1995

I have outlined below a more detailed explanation of the mechanism through which the phenomena I witnessed at Ray Tod's flat appeared. This is with reference to events at the seance with him on 26th July 1995.

In the first place it should be noted that it makes no difference whatever mood I think I'm in - tired, relaxed, expectant etc - the phenomena appear in response to Ray and his state of mind and body. Frequently, and on this occasion, Ray's conversation starts to falter and he appears to lose his train of thought. He will ask me 'what was I saying?' But sometimes as if talking to himself. At the same time I notice (when the lights are full on which they were on this occasion) that the area around Ray goes brighter, becoming almost painful on the eyes. His face becomes fuzzy and the spirits make an appearance. On this occasion Ray's whole body seemed to dissolve, almost as if he was disappearing so that it was possible to look through him and see the area behind. The best analogy I can use is that of a mass of boiling water hanging in the air.

One action that Ray carried out I had not seen him do previously. Instead of raising his arms up to head height which he usually does during the appearance of spirit faces, he stretched each arm out at shoulder height on each side. I can best describe what happened next as an explosion of power, like a car suddenly leaping up several gears at once. The area just above Ray seemed to become brighter and somehow more intense or perhaps thicker or more solid looking.

The face that I saw at this point looked female to me or

someone with prominent cheek bones and a smooth skin. When I discussed this later with Ray he didn't consider that a female person had 'come through' at that point. Anyway, whether male or female (or possibly a male in simple Arab style clothes) I felt as if the spirit was going to leap out and materialise as a complete fully formed being right in front of me. I would say I was stunned, taken aback and had the breath knocked out of me all in one go.

One thing which happens, but which I can't explain occurs as I focus on Ray's face. Heads appear and then it is as if everything goes black. My vision seems to narrow so that I can only see a small area of Ray and then suddenly the whole picture is there again - like a camera snapping a photo.

The most striking face I saw this time came after the first spirit appeared. It was definitely alien and so very clearly visible that you felt you could touch it. It looked so real and solid. It was turnip shaped! And about the same size. The skin looked smooth, but a kind of dirty brown colour. The nose was very thin: pencil thin. It looked humanoid, but definitely not human.

SEANCE SATURDAY 5th AUGUST 1995

The build up of power with Ray has been truly remarkable. One matter that has become apparent to me is that the first face I see is the same on each occasion. He looks like me, but without glasses. I get the impression he is looking at me in a friendly, encouraging manner.

On this occasion, however, the appearance of the spirit faces was not what caught my attention. It was the effect of the phenomena which was the most remarkable feature. The power seemed to build up suddenly and rapidly. It was as if different coloured lights were flashing on and off rapidly so that for what seemed a matter of seconds the room would be dark and in the next instant it would be a kind of purple black. I compared it to ultra violet light being switched on and off, or disco lights flashing rapidly.

I didn't see but 'sensed' a landscape - which was difficult to explain, but on reflection I could have glimpsed a panorama for a second during the period of flashing lights. As this was going on I felt as if the whole room was a mass of excited particles. I had a sensation as if we were literally moving. At this point I didn't know where we might end up and it was only because Ray seemed to decide suddenly to stop it that we went no further. Again, I saw a non-human or 'alien' face. It was white with folds of skin. It looked like a cross between a human and an orangutan.

SEANCE WEDNESDAY 9th AUGUST 1995

On this occasion we spent a considerable amount of time discussing the philosophy of what had been happening through Ray's mediumship and what I had thought about and learned from it. Ray raised the very important point of 'where do I go from here', given what I had witnessed to date. Having seen the spirits and what could be produced through Ray could I go any further? Could I learn any more? And even if I wanted to learn more was I capable of it? I would say that I had (and have) no particular wish to be a medium. I have no doubt that one could train to be one, but my own feeling is that mediums with real ability are born and not made. There can be a lot of self-deception in mediumship and I wouldn't want to waste my own time or anyone else's in an area in which I didn't feel I have any particular ability. My grandmother was a medium, so I have no difficulty in accepting it as genuine.

Ray asked me what difference the experiences with him had made to me. It has, in a literal sense, opened up a new dimension and forced me to reflect on Man's place within the cosmos. Ray has had a long time to mull over what he knows. I've only had a few months. It is difficult to put such a startling revelation into perspective or absorb it in such a relatively short time. It does force you to question Man's significance, given the fact that not only human, but alien spirits appear. The implications of this are challenging. It certainly suggests that searching for alien spacecraft in the skies may be misplaced, as the answer to the UFO puzzle doesn't seem to lie in looking for 'flying saucers' from distant galaxies, but rather in a dimension - or dimensions - which are contemporaneous with our own. These 'aliens' may well occupy the same space as us, but on a different level, or 'vibration'. All that is required is the key to unlock the door.

Ray, however, is the only person I've met (or heard of) who is capable of gaining such a deep entry into this other world, or worlds. I suggested to Ray that at some point he surely must have some public recognition of his mediumship. Ray replied that he will know when the time is right.*

Ray asked me what I could do with what I now knew. There is obviously no easy answer to this. What can any of us do? I believe it is possible to convince people of the existence of the spirit world, and that is an opportunity which shouldn't be ignored even if the numbers are not great. They might be substantial, however, if the matter could be dealt with in a proper forum. If ever Ray decided to take his ability to a wider audience then I'm sure it would be a project in which his spirit friends would have to guide him. I agree that in a sense my own participation could reach an impasse. However, I would like to learn more of the spirits and their world and how they act within it - and many other questions of a similar nature.

As the discussion dominated the evening the phenomena seemed almost incidental! I had noticed on Ray's arm earlier a glowing ball of light. That was well before the phenomena started to appear. The spirit forms which arrived were very strangely formed, but were not very many and I believe their appearance is not at the moment central to a learning experience. The main incident for me was that the room - the whole room - seemed to dissolve. This time there was no shimmering curtain of white light. The whole room seemed one mass of dissolving, moving reddish blobs. It happened so quickly from the time the first face appeared: Peter Cook, again, I'm sure. At times Ray disappeared. I felt as if the whole room was moving and that I was a part of a whole rotating mass of room, furniture and people. It was not a frightening sensation, but certainly an overpowering one. You could unmistakably feel the power at work and realise that you had no ability to stop what was going on. I meant to ask Ray if he sees anything happening to me during these times. During the evening Ray went into the most slumped 'slumber' posture that I've seen him in. His face and body seemed to expand to really fatty proportions and he maintained the longest silence I have known so far.

*Unfortunately, it never came, but maybe Ray realised that such would be the case.

SEANCE WEDNESDAY 30th AUGUST 1995

At this meeting with Ray the main part for me was to try again to bring myself closer to the spirits. I had discussed this with Ray and agreed that it was really the only way to carry out any serious investigation. On this occasion I experienced only a mild fluttering in my stomach. After a while I could feel myself being compressed internally (this was the sensation) until everything seemed to be at head level and it felt as if I would come out of my head at an angle. Why an angle I don't know, but it didn't feel as if I would emerge at my cranium, or temple.

Again, as before, a heavy weight seemed to be pulling me down as if I was going to sink through the floor. A kind of misty whiteness played in front of my eyes (which were, oddly, closed). However, the aspect which struck me most was my inability or difficulty in opening my eyes. It wasn't as if they felt heavy or sticky. It was more as if my own control over opening and shutting them had been impaired. I knew, I think, I could do it if I wished, but I didn't feel I wanted to which was an odd sensation. Before we started I had felt tired and was yawning: afterwards I felt wide awake even though I had been relaxing.

I asked Ray if it was possible to learn to do what he was doing. He replied that it was, but only after training with a medium who was capable of controlling the spirit entities. However, one can train on one's own to a certain extent by meditating and relaxing in a quiet atmosphere while remaining in control of one's faculties.

Ray's ability to turn on and off the presence of the spirits never ceases to astonish me. It isn't something I could ever feel blase about. Each face that appears fascinates me. It is absorbing to be able to see into the worlds inhabited by the spirits. I believe it is in a sense an invitation and an encouragement. It does open your mind to the vastness and unknowable aspects of existence. It is difficult to comprehend its' implications, but somehow you have to try and make sense of it.

SEANCE WEDNESDAY 13th SEPTEMBER 1995

We spent a considerable time discussing (or rather my listening to) Ray's views on religion. On these occasions I'm never sure whether I'm hearing Ray or the spirits' opinions: more likely a mixture. Ray expressed the view that Christianity has a lot to answer for, particularly in respect of the cruelty and injustices of the past. He puts the blame squarely on the shoulders of the 'priests and ministers' and not on the man we know as 'Jesus'. He pointed out aspects of the Bible which do not make any sense in the present day with our scientific knowledge plus advanced technology, and to the contradictions which appear in the Bible.

Ray drew my attention to a connection which had escaped me. He expressed the view that at the same time as many UFO programmes were appearing on television and reports in the media a series of documentaries had been broadcast on Ancient Egypt. Ray seemed to suggest that these were somehow linked. He also pointed out that there was a connection between the layout of the pyramids which correspond to the position of the constellation Orion and the fact that the Dogon tribe of Mali in West Africa knew about the constellation and in particular the existence of the star Sirius B over 5,000 years ago, long before modern man had discovered it.*As Ray pointed out three major religions originated in the Middle East. WHY?! Could the origins of Christianity and the older religions of Ancient Egypt be connected with outer space? After all, from what I have seen with Ray, there are spirit aliens too.

As the evening wore on my eyes became heavier and heavier. There was no way I could keep them open. All the time I'm with Ray now the faces seem to appear or about to appear. Eventually, to my relief, Ray turned down the lights though I could still see him and the surroundings in every detail. Peter Cook then appeared and one or two others. I felt forced to close my eyes when Ray closed his. I then felt some fluttering in my stomach and my eyes seemed to become heavier as if I was sinking deeper and deeper. After a while I felt as if part of me was trying to burst out of my body - as if I was trying to leave the corporeal behind, but something was holding me back. At this point I felt tightness all over my skin as if it was being physically stretched.

Ray then came over and placed his hands on my head. I immediately felt more relaxed and the internal agitation and desire to leave my body seemed to evaporate. (At some point I forced myself into a more comfortable position almost as if I had been made to.)

I don't know how long Ray stayed beside me, but at some point I felt that instead of slipping out of my body, a force of some kind was slipping into my chest. My throat became very dry and it was as if someone was trying to make me speak and I knew that if I had let myself I would have said something to Ray. I could feel my lips moving. My whole body became very heavy. I felt that I could take control at any time, but it would require effort on my part. In fact, the effort was substantial because when I did 'come

31

back' I still felt dazed and almost as if I didn't want to emerge. The effect was only really broken when Ray himself ended the contact and I immediately felt then as if I'd been unplugged from an electric socket.

*I was aware of the mystery surrounding the Dogon's knowledge of Sirius and the scepticism expressed by some writers as to how they had gained this knowledge. Ray though appeared to accept it at face value.

SEANCE WEDNESDAY 4th OCTOBER 1995

At this get together it seemed for most of the evening that there was going to be no appearance of the spirit faces. Ray and I spent a considerable part of the time discussing what I was doing and at times there was some frank exchanges on matters. However, even during the discussion I could see faces trying hard to materialise and from time to time the space around Ray appeared to be breaking up, or perhaps 'agitated' is a better way of putting it.

When spirits appeared they did so suddenly and with tremendous clarity - all the shape and configuration of a face you would see in this world you can see in these faces. I must mention one which simply astounded me. At first I thought it was a gorilla, but as it became clearer I saw that it looked remarkably human, obviously highly intelligent and I could make out the top of a coat or covering of some kind which must mean that I saw the torso. The 'being' had flowing black hair, but of the texture of a gorilla's, swept back from the head.

I should say that during all this time the room was in full bright light and I was sitting only a few feet from Ray. I also found that the light was not hurting my eyes as it usually does. One aspect I should have noted earlier is that before the spirit faces appear there is an increase in the intensity of white light.

I was truly astounded by what was happening to Ray. The jumper he was wearing became an intense pattern of brown and white zig-zag patterns. It was a spectacular sight. Then Ray himself began to dematerialise. His head appeared to shrink until it became a white blob. He no longer seemed to be sitting in a chair a few feet away from me! The chair itself seemed to be disappearing. The power and agitated air just grew and grew in strength. The whole room appeared to be dissolving and I did have a sense of being on the edge of a remarkable insight although something over which I had no control. I must say, however, that at no time did I feel threatened.

Perhaps the most noticeable part of all is Ray's ability to bring the phenomena to a halt in almost an instant. This demonstrates that whoever, or whatever, is working with Ray does have confidence in him (and vice versa) and respect for the man and I, for my part, trust those who are involved with him. There is an incredible power to be seen here and I say again it is truly awe inspiring.

One other face which I must mention was an 'Egyptian', but it looked like a statue rather than a real person. It was a thin face with high cheekbones and wore archetypal Egyptian headwear associated with the ruling class.

SEANCE WEDNESDAY 25th OCTOBER 1995

Ray and I spent a considerable amount of time discussing religion. The views that he expressed left little doubt that he (and those who speak through him) had no time for Christianity and not much for other religions either. Buddhism, however, seemed to be less harshly regarded than other faiths. Ray's main criticism was that religion *per se* has caused a huge amount of bloodshed and that the hypocrisy of religious leaders knows no bounds. Naturally, they want to keep the masses in thrall and, therefore, oppose anything that would break up their 'operation' such as the alleged appearance of spirits. As Ray claimed, he might well have been burnt as a witch three hundred years ago.

Ray told me that he was determined to avoid publicity as he believed it only cheapened his mediumship. I asked Ray how he thought the spirits spent their time and he replied that they pass the time as we do here*. Although this might seem like common sense I find it rather surprising. Ray does emphasise the power of the spirits and their ability to know your thoughts - the last of which I find rather disconcerting.

On this occasion the spirit face that appeared initially was the one I nearly always see first now. He looked a bit like me with grey hair, short, about my age and clear lines under his eyes. Once again I found it impossible to keep my eyes open and had to close them. I found myself drifting and compared with the week before I did feel as if I was about to float out of my body although seemed to be held back. Soon after closing my eyes I felt a sharp pain at my forehead though it did not last for very long. Instead of complete darkness I could make out with my eyes closed trees and mountains in the background. It wasn't crystal clear: more like shadows, but I could be sure of what I'd seen. Eventually, I opened my eyes feeling dazed, but gradually becoming wide awake.

*The Swedish medium Emanuel Swedenborg (born 1688) said and wrote the same in several books, giving detailed descriptions of the buildings to be found in the 'next life'.

SEANCE THURSDAY 2nd NOVEMBER 1995

As had been the trend in recent weeks, Ray and I spent considerable time discussing the philosophy of Spiritualism and Ray's role in revealing the phenomena. Frequently, during the conversation I am uncertain as to who is speaking: Ray or someone through him? I would say that at times Ray's views of religion or rather the way it has corrupted the Earth become very clear and put over with such force that the opinion expressed seems to come from 'beyond Ray'. I'm not sure whether his views were completely forged before he made such close contact with the spirit world, but I think they have been confirmed by what he has learnt rather than led him to that conclusion.

I would have to agree (I don't see what other conclusion you can come to) that if aliens and humans are mixing together in the 'after life' then all Earthly religions have got it wrong. That means, of course, that much of the basis of present life and a lot of the structures set up by humans are complete nonsense. I don't feel that this would be easily accepted even by the best educated people and certainly not by those whose position is based on being at the top of these structures, for example, world leaders. So what is there to be gained by revealing to the world what Ray can do?

Having thought about it at length I still have no idea what the answer is. Personally, I'm quite happy to witness phenomena literally out of this world, and, considering the implications, there's enough to tax your brain for the rest of your life. It seems beyond belief that given the ability to reveal what Ray can demonstrate that it will remain hidden away. A circle of people know or have heard about what Ray can do, but the implications are of such significance that people may respond by rejecting it. However, I stand by what I've seen though I sometimes have to mentally pinch myself and say, 'Ron, it WAS there.' There is no doubt that by being with Ray my own thoughts on these matters and my own awareness has increased dramatically. It can be unsettling and no one likes to be unsettled, but it is also mind-stretching. I would like to get closer, but it is difficult to abandon self-control and accept something that is really so immense.

SEANCE THURSDAY 30th NOVEMBER 1995

On this occasion Ray and I again spent a considerable amount of time discussing the philosophy of Spiritualism. I am now quite familiar with Ray's - or the 'spirits' - views of religion and this is clearly an important issue. Obviously, not only are existing faiths to be seen as wrong, but they are blocking our perception of what is the real way forward. I think that this is meant both in a spiritual and in an earthly sense, that is that we cannot learn more about our spiritual

35

selves and we can do nothing to benefit the Earth until we understand that the true revelation isn't to be found in current religion. Ray again emphasised the links between ancient Egypt and current interest in UFOs. We are all part of a vast universe in which there are different types of beings - as exemplified by the spirits that appear through Ray. On this occasion, for example, I saw a grey-faced 'ape' just like the fresh-faced black one I'd seen previously. Man can only go forward if he realises these truths. I saw coloured lights around Ray which he explained as the presence of spirits.

I could not keep my eyes open again and felt forced to shut them. I felt that drifting, relaxed sensation, but also intense agitation. I felt the urge to speak, but didn't. When I 'came to' I felt wide awake again.

SEANCE THURSDAY 14th DECEMBER 1995

After a year of meeting with Ray and experiencing a range of astonishing phenomena and insights, it seemed impossible that at our last meeting of 1995 anything new could happen. However, as ever, the spirits never fail to surprise you and put you in your place.

Ray had been pointing out to me that one's experiences could reach a plateau and that it was necessary to think about what had happened over the past months and consider where I wanted to go with it. I responded that as he is the medium, I am dependant on where he wants to go. I have had some limited experiences on my own, but there will be no further development without Ray's (and the spirits!) assistance.

Ray again emphasised his opposition to Christianity - Christmas was fast approaching - and its detrimental effect on human development. If aliens have been visiting us for thousands of years we are, indeed, low down on the tree of development and all religions are misguided. Man is not the centre of the universe and, in fact, may be in a position of being no more than tolerated by other species.

Ray continues to be very focussed on ancient Egypt and its interactions with visitors from other parts of the universe. He has an interesting conception of what the pyramids represent which I won't reveal as it is Ray's idea, but I believe it does offer an explanation of the mystery of why these buildings were erected.

I should say that Ray does not deny the role of figures such as Jesus, only the interpretation of their activities and origins by religion. This brings me on to my most astonishing experience. I was starting to see spirit faces when all of a sudden this incredible visage appeared. It had a smile on its lips and short golden coloured hair cut with a fringe in the Greek style. I was dumbfounded as I instantly recognised this figure as the ancient Greek god ZEUS. He looked at me knowingly as if challenging me to recognise him. I must have gasped out his name or else he knew that I had recognised him because the effect on Ray was astonishing. It was as if he had been hit by a sledgehammer. His head slumped on to his chest as if he was in a deep sleep. I was still muttering to myself in astonishment when Ray 'surfaced'. Clearly, Ray too had been surprised by the intensity of the reaction. 'They like to be recognised', he said wryly.

What added to my surprise was that I had been thinking about ZEUS on the journey to Ray's house although I certainly had not mentioned it to Ray. I would like to make it clear that ZEUS appeared to me in bright light (that is, full room light) when I was only a few feet from Ray. The sighting only lasted seconds, but it has burnt an image on my mind and I find myself thinking constantly about it and considering its significance. ZEUS was regarded as the father of the ancient Greek pantheon of gods (his equivalent in ancient Rome was Jupiter). The oracle of ZEUS was the oldest of all the ancient oracles. The appearance of ZEUS could be interpreted symbolically, but it could also represent a spirit of a real being. Given all the spirits that have appeared, I have to accept that it was that of a real person. Ray, I should add, never seems fazed by anything that happens and takes it all in his stride.

One last point: as Ray said, 'Do you still think that to see spirits you have to be born with the ability?' I think the answer has to be 'no'.

SEANCE THURSDAY 11th JANUARY 1996

This was our first meeting of 1996 and some weeks since we had last got together. It was, as well, almost a year since I had first met Ray. There is, however, always something different no matter how often I visit. I sat in my usual chair facing Ray and almost immediately sensed something out of the ordinary. The atmosphere of the room struck me as not what I had become used to. I was chatting to Ray at this time so I didn't mention it to him for the moment. Meanwhile, Ray asked me if I had seen the Paul McKenna show*. I had only caught the last few minutes so agreed to watch the whole show which Ray had on video. It was extraordinary to watch a Russian pull a forty ton train with wires hooked to his arms. One might well ask, 'Was that man human?'

After the video was finished I sat chatting to Ray for a few minutes, but it was clear he was distracted. I began to quantify what I felt was different. The atmosphere struck me as thicker and more dense than usual. That is the only way I can think to describe it. As these thoughts went through my head and Ray was talking the room began to dissolve and spirit faces made an appearance. Ray then said to me, 'there's something different tonight'.We had both sensed the difference independently. Ray then stated that this had happened previously when there had been a break in the spirit presence. Now it was as if the floodgates had opened. I can only compare it to a power surge. It was so strong that I felt physically sick the way I had felt at the start of my meetings with Ray. Thinking back to the present meeting, I realize now that I was in a daze.

It was fascinating to watch Ray. It seemed to me as if the

extra power was having an effect on him too. He rarely seems surprised at what happens with the spirits, but he did seem a little taken aback on this occasion. Around the room there shone an intense display of lights, burning bright like white flames in a furnace. I have seen Ray dissolve before my eyes before, only a few feet from me, but this time it happened in an instant till there was only a messy bundle to be seen, coloured a kind of dull cream. All the area round about us seemed to be disappearing too and I noticed, for the first time ever, that my own hands were glowing. I wondered to myself, 'where are we going to end up?'

I would state categorically that at no point did I sense any menace or threat. The feeling that surrounded me was one of great enthusiasm: the power kept surging again and again. The spirits would not leave Ray alone. At one point Ray raised an arm (afterwards he told me he could not keep it down) and an outline of flame-like colours was running around his fingers.

Spirit faces appeared, but one I distinctly remember was alien. It looked like the ape-faced one, but thinner and a bit more of a humanoid appearance, prominent cheekbones and eyes. The skin looked a kind of pea-green colour although that may have been a product of the exceptionally thick atmosphere in the room. The presence of this spirit created an incredibly powerful aura. He was not threatening us, however. He undoubtedly had presence, as Ray put it, 'a person to be reckoned with.' There is no doubt in my mind that this spirit was telling us that he was doing us a favour by showing himself. I had the feeling of strength yet wisdom and fairness all in a matter of seconds. I felt that, personally, I had proceeded further into another dimension than ever before. However, the more I see the less I think people will believe me.

I experienced a few headaches during this and Ray said, 'tell them to stop it.' I did and it worked.

*Popular stage and television hypnotist of the time

Ray Tod in the 1990s.

The author at West Montgomery Place, Edinburgh.

SEANCE THURSDAY 8th FEBRUARY 1996

I continued to feel that there was a strange atmosphere in Ray's living room. As I wrote the previous month the atmosphere which followed the break we'd had between December 1995 and January 1996 was electric and somehow more dense. This time it was not as intense as the previous time, but still markedly different from that which I had experienced throughout 1995.

However, why should things be different from 1995? The answer must be in Ray. He has mentioned in the past that the 'power' will build up as we continue to 'sit'. Ray has always appeared so much in touch with the spirits that he seems as much a part of their world as he is of ours. I would agree with Ray that over the past year the 'force' has increased tremendously and shows no sign of abating.

I am also aware that my own sensitivity has increased significantly over the past year. There is an old saying about getting too 'close to the sun' and that is how it feels sometime. The implications of what I have seen are astonishing so that one's mind shuts off and only lets a little trickle through at a time. Which brings me to this particular meeting with Ray. The one incident which stands out in my memory was the sight of a blazing column of white, orange and reddish light which stretched from Ray's right shoulder as I faced him and reached almost to the ceiling.

I had a vague recollection of seeing spirit faces, but this one moment seemed to dominate my thoughts and I have been unable to get it out of my mind. I have mulled over what it might be or represent. The column of light was just behind Ray or could have been attached to him. It might have been a particularly powerful spirit associated with Ray. It could have been an opening into another dimension. One that I had not been aware of. These are the thoughts that have gone through my mind since this incident. It was as if I was being 'forced' to contemplate this particular 'vision' and that everything else had been held back at this meeting to encourage me to think about it carefully.

Somehow I sense that it will appear again and that it has a significance to my own understanding of what is happening with Ray.

SEANCE SUNDAY 18th FEBRUARY 1996

No matter how many times I have visited Ray, the spirits have never failed to surprise me. There is always something different, almost as if you are being led deliberately further up a road to some unknown destination. How and why? Many times I have found myself in a state of astonishment and almost disbelief. At times it becomes almost too much to take in. No wonder our friends in the universe hesitate from approaching us directly. Now for the meeting.

To begin with Ray and I sat talking for a while then in the middle of something which Ray was saying a whole range of spirit faces including 'alien' ones appeared. However even this became unimportant as the face of 'Zeus' materialised as it had once before. His features looked as if they had been chiselled from marble, they looked so fine. Yet I could sense that he was very much alive. His face was impassive but friendly and astonishingly life-like. This was no sculpture. It was not exactly the same face as I had seen before but in a different aspect. He stared straight at me and I certainly experienced a feeling of understanding and warmth. It was as if he knew that I had started to appreciate his significance to the planet and man's development. He did not have to say 'I am Zeus' because his thoughts were implanted in my head as soon as he appeared. His image seemed to be floating in the air completely separate from Ray. His hair was short and his nose and cheekbones prominent.

There is always a gap between the appearance of the spirit faces. They come in a rush sometimes, like a crowd at a railway station. Then the power seems to run down for a short time. During this occasion Ray appeared to be in communication with the spirits and asked me if I felt okay. I told him that I had sinusitis. He said he was going to put his hand on my head. He said that the spirits wanted to draw me closer to them. He did not explain why.

I closed my eyes and immediately began to feel a surge of power going through my body. It wasn't painful but was uncomfortable. It was as if a heavy weight was pressing down on me and was so intense that I had to stop myself from getting out of my seat. However, this passed and I felt myself floating upwards. At one point I sensed Ray standing beside me and felt my elbow nudging him. I was amazed when I opened my eyes and saw him still sitting in his chair. He just smiled and said that he had put his hand on my head but had not moved from his seat. Strange? Ray asked me what I remembered and I said 'just dazed!' He then said that the spirits had imparted knowledge to me that I would remember later. During one part of the evening I saw a second arm and hand behind Ray's right arm. Was this the arm that had touched my head?

POSTSCRIPT: As I was driving home the face of 'Zeus' appeared in my mind so clearly that I could see his face in the road in front of me and then I realised I was having a migraine and could not see ahead of me to drive properly. I pulled over to a lay-by. It was as if I had been warned.

SEANCE SUNDAY 10th MARCH 1996

Ray and I spent considerable time discussing various UFO matters and although in my bones I felt that the spirits would come through I did have doubts. Occasionally, I have to try and convince myself that there are no spirits and that it is all down to imagination: if I say to myself 'I won't see them' they won't turn up. They always do though which shows that the matter is not under my control or influence. Ray usually turns the lights down (although they are still on - just a bit dimmer) but on this occasion he asked me to do it as his eyes were stinging.

I have increasing difficulty in remembering the spirit faces that appear and instead recall particular incidents. Ray has had to jog my memory about one or two things which I have mentioned to him shortly after they happened, but slipped my mind because I had been thinking about other incidents. At one point an Egyptian face appeared. It was broad and round, but the most striking point was the straight black hair. I immediately identified it with the pictures of ancient Egyptians depicted constructing the pyramids.

Ray's right hand was glowing as if there was a pink force field or aura forming a duplicate hand beside his own. The living-room kept moving around until I felt dizzy. I had clocked this effect on previous occasions, but on this occasion it seemed especially noticeable. The whole shape of the room appeared to change. The door seemed to come in at right angles to where we were sitting so that it was parallel to our chairs. From beneath the door at floor level an intense bright streak of light could be seen. I have not witnessed this before. Overall the whole room looked to have shrunk to about a third of its size - it felt claustrophobic.

However, the key incident for me was one which I didn't mention to Ray at the time. When he reads this it will be the first he has heard it. I didn't mention it because I wanted to be sure I wasn't imagining it. Ray mentioned to me that the spirits wished to heal me. In fact, I wouldn't say that I had noticed anything in particular happening to me. I had been suffering the effects of sinusitis at the back of my nose and throat. It had been irritating me and I knew it hadn't cleared up. As I sat opposite Ray who was at that point in contact with the spirits, I felt the interior of my mouth and nose start to tingle. It was a very strong feeling. I could feel the irritation start to go away. I don't know how long it lasted. Maybe a minute or so, but by the end the irritation had gone. There was no doubt in my mind that my complaint had dissipated in a very short time. I was amazed because I had only read about such things, but had never experienced it or felt that I ever would. I hadn't asked for it to happen yet it had, suddenly and intensely. I am not sure whether it was because I was in the vicinity of something both powerful and good or it was pure luck on my part. What to me was the most astonishing thing was that the tingling sensation was so localised and was felt just in those areas which had been annoying me.

SEANCE THURSDAY 21st MARCH 1996

Ray and I spent a considerable part of our meeting discussing a wide range of matters including the production of 'Phenomenal News'* for which Ray had various suggestions. During this part of the evening I had the distinct feeling that the spirits were trying very hard to come through, but it is an indication of Ray's control that he can stop the spirits materialising if he so wants. All this time the atmosphere around me did feel heavy and I found myself yawning, a sure sign of the presence of the spirits. However, I have noticed that in recent weeks I have been feeling less tired at Ray's as if I am getting used to the thicker atmosphere.

Once Ray allowed the spirits through the phenomena appeared rapidly and dramatically. The walls of the room gave the appearance of moving from side to side, or, alternatively, the area in which we were sitting was and everything else was standing still. The space where Ray and I were sitting started to dissolve. One spirit face that I always see first and who heralds the start of the phenomena appeared and soon after Ray started to disappear before my eyes. For a period I could see nothing in front of me but a mass of distortion. It was like being caught in the middle of a 'white out' except it was more the colour of pea-green soup. There were no reference points and seeing nothing but the distortion, I did feel a moment of concern.

Ray then re-emerged and the room again became visible, but all around it was as if there were batteries of flashing lights. I mentioned once before the similarity of the phenomena to ultra violet light with dark and light about equal. When I write 'dark' I don't mean black, but more a dull colour. The light appeared as if it was layered with varying tones of colour in different parts. It seemed to me that we were travelling further into a different dimension from that I had experienced previously and I asked myself, 'where is this going to end?' When it stopped which it did quickly, I felt exhausted and physically disturbed. It took me a while to feel normal again.

One other point I noticed was that as the phenomena gets underway the walls of the room which are light start to darken as if the room is encased by a physical presence (a 'blanket') which masks the light.

* 'Phenomenal News' was the magazine published by 'Scottish Earth Mysteries Research', a group I inaugurated and chaired. The magazine editor was Viv Alexander.

SEANCE WEDNESDAY 27th MARCH 1996

On this occasion events took a different tack. By the end of the evening I felt that I had been almost as involved as Ray is in the proceedings. Before the phenomena manifested I did clarify one part of the mechanism with Ray and this is that the disturbance within the room involves him alone. When I see a gateway opening with multicoloured lights and other phenomena it is Ray who is moving into another dimension. I am really only a spectator to what is taking place. It is strange to think that Ray is not fully aware of what is happening around him. I'm not sure why this should be the case. It may be that I am seeing the disturbance between the two dimensions as they come into harmony whereas the person through whom this is taking place has only an internal sensation.

Ray explained that what is transpiring at these times is that the vibrations of the spirit world and our world are coming into harmony. According to Ray the Earth's vibrations are faster than that of spirit and that what happened was that through his physical body the Earth's vibrations were slowed down. He is, in a sense, a gate through which the two dimensions can meet. I'm surprised that I can remember all this because the phenomena left me

47

in a stupefied state this time. Ray said, 'you'll get used to it', but at the time of writing I'm not convinced. You have to be impressed by Ray's determination and tough mindedness to cope so easily with very powerful forces. I think that there are very few people who could carry out this kind of mediumship (even if they had the ability) and at the same time keep their equilibrium.

Although at our meeting the previous week I had written that I found it easier to keep my eyes open, almost in response, I found it impossible this time. As Ray opened up to the spirits, I could feel their presence sinking in to me. I could hardly make out any spirits as Ray's face seemed to be continually out of focus. He then closed his eyes and I found that I could not keep mine open. When I did close them I rapidly sank into a deep state of 'waking sleep' (it feels like an apt description). It is a strange condition and so hard to describe unless you have experienced it. I was aware of my surroundings, but at the same time I felt completely isolated as if suspended in a black hole of nothingness. Your mind is a complete blank even though you feel very much alive. On this occasion, at one point, seemingly meaningless images flashed through my mind for a split second. One, I think, was of a ghostly train. They didn't appear to have any particular meaning.

During this state I was aware of Ray taking extraordinarily deep breaths as if he was sucking in a whole roomful of air. My eyes seemed to open of their own accord and I saw Ray with his head slumped forward breathing in for a huge length of time. His head and body looked about twice their normal size. He did not seem to be exhaling for anything like the amount of time he was breathing in and I'm not sure I heard Ray breathe out at all.

My eyes closed again and I was aware of a heavy yet agitated feeling within my body. At one point, I felt as if I was drifting off (I mean physically) to another plane. All of this was having a strong physical effect on me. When I eventually 'came out' (only after Ray had 'closed the door' on the spirits), I was totally drained and exhausted. I could hardly speak sensibly and my mind was not focusing. Ray said that these experiences invigorated him whereas I was all at sea. That night I did have a disturbed sleep which has not really happened to me before.

The power that comes through Ray is astonishing. It not only has an effect on him, but me too even though I am only a spectator. There must be something about Ray which while it allows contact to be made, nullifies the effect it should have on him. I don't think that my mind or body could sustain that impact for any length of time. Yet he can do it for 30 minutes or more at one go and emerge from it as if nothing had happened. It is one of the marvels of all time and you think, 'where can it all end?' What might be learnt from such contact? Ray can go much, much further. I think he is only at the beginning.

SEANCE FRIDAY 26th APRIL 1996 (possibly 1995)*

The impression that stood out for me this time was of a grey-haired person - not old, not even middle-aged. It looked like someone who had prematurely turned grey. At another point, another grey-haired person appeared looking very similar to the one mentioned above. The hair on both occasions was very prominent - thick and bushy. On the second occasion, the face appeared to surmount a collar that looked like that of a soldier's uniform. Lots of spirits appeared momentarily. The person with a high forehead and lined face appeared at one point. I should add that the grey-haired spirit appeared very strongly to me - the nearest I have seen to a solid face.

One thing I have realised is that one of the first signs that the phenomena is about to start is the appearance of a dark ring like a monocle around Ray's face. Ray's features become harsher and craggier. I think I'd noticed this on previous occasions, but its' significance has only just struck me. On this occasion, Ray said he'd seen a face around me, of a woman, which seemed to resemble my father's mother, that is broad faced and in her 50s.+

Again, I noticed that the shimmering effect was less than previously. Ray materialised the faces in bright light. I could see them, but I found it a strain on the eyes compared with the dimmer light.

* I could not find a typed up version of this seance - I've no idea why I didn't type it up. Nor am I sure about the year. It says '1994' on the handwritten version which can't be right. Going by the narrative I think it fits better into 1996.

+ My paternal grandmother died in her fifties

SEANCE WEDNESDAY 8th MAY 1996

Ray and I met on 8th May after a few weeks break. It was odd but I noticed that the atmosphere was 'fresher' as if it had been renewed. I actually didn't expect anything to happen. I don't know why exactly, but I think because in the past the phenomena seemed to build up gradually. It no longer does and seems to rush rather than seep in. In spite of what I have seen, I still have a worry that perhaps I will no longer be able to see the phenomena. Yes, I am starting to feel as if I will lose old friends if they don't appear.

As on several occasions I could see the people almost bursting to come through and Ray alone preventing them. I think Ray is unique. Maybe there is only one and only ever will be one medium with his ability. If there is only one 'Ray' why should that be the case? It is a genuine puzzle. Anyway on this occasion I witnessed further surprises. The first face I saw, however, was not a surprise. It was that person who always appears, with short grey hair, with a contemporary look and with a wry smile as if to say 'don't you recognise me?' I don't recognise him, but feel I should.

The next face I did recognise. It was my grandfather's, but aged in his 40s. Ray meanwhile was talking about Amen (Ancient Egypt), Zeus (Ancient Greece) and Odin (Norse). Immediately afterwards, Odin appeared. He looked like drawings of him that you might see anywhere with short hair, a trim beard and a sharp tight-boned face. He had a strong presence. How did I know it was Odin? Because of the characteristic face and the name 'Odin' that came into my mind when he appeared. I realised that Odin's face came as a representation, but he appeared in a way that I would recognise to confirm (I think) that he knew I was interested in him and what he stood for. With Odin I had the impression of a tough, sharp edged, unforgiving person. To his friends, just, but ruthless to his enemies.

I noted some interesting aspects of these events:

(a) when faces materialise they do so in two ways. Sometimes they seem to flow over Ray's face and appear gradually. On other occasions Ray's head seems to disappear in a brown and green sludge, almost as if it had been sucked into a hole, and then a face emerges.

(b) I saw something I've always wanted to see, but never have. This was spirit lights, dozens of them, like fireflies floating around the room. It was an incredible sight which I hope I will see again.

SEANCE WEDNESDAY 15th MAY 1996

The atmosphere felt noticeably different from previous occasions. I guessed that this was because [a female friend of Ray's] was present. He had informed me that she had clairvoyant abilities. I had not met her till this point. When I later mentioned to Ray that the atmosphere seemed different he indicated to me that this was because 'like attracts like'. By this he meant that [his friend] attracted to her similar characters, or perhaps the types she wanted to meet (or wanted to meet her): in the same way I saw Winston Churchill, Peter Sellers, Peter Cook, Odin, Zeus etc . Politicians, actors and gods! Ray also reminded me that previously I thought that [name deleted] influenced the arrival of spirits, but it was simply that the 'like attracts like' formula had been working on that occasion.

I did see several faces, but in terms of the phenomena's mechanism, I became aware of thick areas of light in different parts of the room, as if 'something' was trying to form. It was bright light contained within a definite area with a thicker and different coloured rim. These weren't on the ground, but were higher up: in one case above Ray's chair. Sometimes you think something is going to happen, but it doesn't as if you suddenly lose concentration, or lose a 'link'. While I was seeing the spirits - and I was looking face on to Ray at the time - [name deleted] was seeing faces emerging from the side of Ray's head. [Name deleted] was sitting at an angle, slightly further away than me, at around 45 degrees from Ray. I thought I might find her presence distracting, but I didn't. I did find it hard to remember the faces I had witnessed, but that of Odin's kept reappearing in my mind -almost as if he was saying 'you must remember me.'

SEANCE WEDNESDAY 14th AUGUST 1996

I met Ray after an absence of a few weeks though I had been at his house during the visit of Bob and Cecilia Dean*. I would say first of all that during the latter's visit the phenomena appeared to me to be very strong. Ray's head disappeared from my view even though I was sitting side on and not directly in front as usual. Needless to say there was plenty of lighting.

Returning to the visit on the 14th: the phenomena was again powerful. All around Ray I could see shimmering lights. The spirits as ever appeared to be bursting to come through. Several spirits appeared including a distinctly alien one. It was grey in colour with wrinkled skin and hairless. It was a large face. The spirits gave the impression of being knowing and intelligent. However, as I was watching, Ray's head disappeared and in its' place there was a grey mass, even that disappeared to be followed by his whole person and the seat he was sitting on. It was as if I was looking into utter blackness. I would have to admit that I felt a moment of concern. What's going on?' I asked myself. Then Ray reappeared. However, as I watched, his head turned into a silver-coloured mask. Or perhaps a better description would be that of a silver-coloured balloon, but almost two-dimensional. It was completely featureless.

I could feel the power increasing and it was as if Ray and I were travelling down a tunnel. The world about us seemed to close in and darken. The atmosphere was one of agitation and movement. I looked down at my hands and saw that they appeared to be glowing pink. My shirt where my hands were resting was glowing white, but I did not have a white-coloured shirt on: it was dark. The area around us seemed to go from dark to light and then to dark again as if someone was flicking a light switch on and off. But the thing I noticed was that somehow the atmosphere and this flickering phenomenon seemed to be slowing down as if either Ray and I were altering time or, alternatively, everything else was following a different time. Interestingly, I did not feel tired during the evening and, on the contrary, stimulated.

*See Appendix II

SEANCE WEDNESDAY 21st AUGUST 1996
When I meet with Ray, the experience seems to divide into two broad categories. One is where I observe various phenomena: the other is where the experience has a direct physical effect on me. One further factor is that on occasion my memory of events seems to be partly blocked so that on some visits I come out with a very vivid recollection of what took place whilst at other times the picture seems obscure, one more of feeling than actual images in your memory.

Today my experience fell into the latter category. I should maybe expand on my comments in the previous paragraph. The recollection of events may be hazy overall, but there tends to be a strong focus on one particular part of the evening. I can remember on this occasion seeing faces, but I can't visualise them clearly. What I did experience was an intense sleepiness as I was sitting watching Ray 'doing the business' as he calls it. I know that this feeling is no accident as I had commented the previous week that nowadays I rarely felt tired during these visits. I had congratulated myself on fully adjusting to the presence of these powerful forces. Speaking too soon!

It is hard to describe the intensity of feeling that comes over you. It is tiredness in that it has the physical symptoms of a weariness you feel you can't resist. Your eyes close almost against your will. Your body relaxes. Yet your mind stays absolutely alert. More alert than ever. This leads me to think that the relaxation of your body is part of a design to focus your mind. A heaviness seems to descend on you which (according to Ray) is spirit taking over your physical form. In my case I felt again an urge to speak to Ray as if some other person had taken over my voice box. It was a message for him and the message came into my head at the same time. I felt that whoever was wishing to deliver that message did not have enough control over my physical body to be able to complete it. During this time I could see that peculiar blackness in front of my eyes with tantalising shapes appearing from time to time. I should say that I 'went under' during the time that Ray had closed his eyes. He wasn't looking at me at this time. I 'came out' to find Ray making circular movements with his hands which seem to have the effect of bringing me back fully into the material world

SEANCE WEDNESDAY 4th SEPTEMBER 1996

I would have to put down my experience at Ray's, on this occasion, as one of the most remarkable of my life. It all started off fairly quietly. He and I were chatting about various things including the poltergeist incidents we had been involved in up north, at Johnshaven [a fishing village on Scotland's east coast]. Ray had told me that he didn't really feel like engaging with the spirits as he had a bit of a cold. I said I could appreciate that he might not feel like doing anything today. I noticed, however, that the spirits were trying to come through and, from time to time almost did, but Ray seemed to be keeping them under control. I was feeling quite relaxed and although I always liked seeing the spirits, I appreciated that I'd been lucky to see what I'd experienced so far. I had, however, sensed that what I had seen was just a prelude to what could happen. That there was a huge amount yet to be revealed. I have no doubt that Ray holds the key to unravelling a whole lot of mysteries.

Around 10.45pm by which time we were normally turning our minds to ending the evening, Ray seemed to decide that perhaps things might happen after all. He turned down the lights and put on one of the relaxing tapes of music that he plays. Immediately, faces started to appear, but events soon went a lot further. Ray himself disappeared as he sometimes does. But again, this was merely the start of a deeper journey. The whole room now started to dissolve in a most rapid and agitated manner. I sensed that we were journeying further than I had gone before and I realised too that I was not nervous about it. I wanted to go on. I was practically begging the spirits to take us further. Ray seemed more affected by the power than I have ever seen him before, but still in control. Suddenly we seemed to be 'right through'. I really felt that we had arrived at another world. The sensation was incredible. It was utterly relaxing and pleasant. I said to myself, 'I don't want to come back from here'. I felt that I could have stayed there.

How can I describe it visually? It was like being in a pleasant, green-coloured environment. It was as if the air around you was moving in slight waves. It was distorted a little bit giving the sensation you were in the middle of something that was floating and you were looking out on your surroundings. Like being in thin, crystal-clear water and gazing from that into an area beyond. I was staggered by this experience. We had moved into another place which existed on the same spot we had been sitting at seconds before, but was different. I said to Ray afterwards, 'No one would believe us.'

SEANCE WEDNEDAY 25th SEPTEMBER 1996

As I watched Ray's face change, Ray continued to talk. On this occasion he was talking about the effect he had on my dowsing rods while at Roslyn chapel. As I have reported several times, these changes to his face take place in full light while he chats, holding a normal conversation. It is almost as if the spirits are gradually bringing Ray into correspondence with their own world. Sometimes Ray appears to slow down as if the 'other world' is having a powerful effect on his thoughts, but he is always fully aware of this world (the one we inhabit).

As on past occasions, Ray's face started to disappear and then other faces appeared. His breathing became deeper and deeper until it seemed at times as if he was hardly respiring at all. The gaps between breaths were very noticeable. It is almost as if his body metabolism was slowing down or at least changing in some way. Ray's situation during this time was not static. It appeared to fluctuate. For some minutes he seemed to be deep within the spirit realm then for a while more in this world and then deeper in contact with spirit again.

While I was watching Ray I kept seeing a flashing blue light to the right side of me as I faced him. I had not seen this phenomenon before. All around the room was an intense white light - almost blinding in its intensity. Ray dissolved and I kept seeing a face which was especially clear. It was solid and not like the ectoplasmic faces that I usually see although, as I think I have written before, the faces that appear have been looking more and more solid. The face was golden-haired and Zeus-like. The face of Zeus has appeared on many occasions now.

For a while the faces faded. Then Ray raised his arms and opened them wide and the effect was the equivalent of a power surge. Ray started dissolving again. His chest glowed bright white. Ray's right hand was glowing white too and his left hand glowing red. I should add that at each deep breath that Ray took, the power seemed to build up. At the start of his contact with the spirits, I saw the face which I have seen many times and which I recognise as that of my grandfather. I also saw a nineteenth century figure with half moon spectacles, and so, perhaps, the figure may have been of a later date and given the appearance of an older era than it actually was. The tendency has been for me to see less faces, but more phenomena. Zeus I saw in both a younger and older version. The whole room was dissolving and swaying so that I really began to feel dizzy.

During this time I noticed that on the wall above Ray's head there had appeared a pyramid shape. It was three dimensional. There was a door on the window in the pyramid with a red glow behind it. On another part of the wall, to the right of the pyramid as I was looking at it, appeared the outline of the Egyptian cat god which Ray later informed me was called Bastet [spelt variously]. The pyramid was about the size of a hand and I could sense the desert all around it. The cat figure was two to three feet in length

SEANCE SUNDAY 20th OCTOBER 1996

I sat down and talked with Ray in the usual way covering a variety of subjects. I sensed that nothing much was going to happen because I got the impression that Ray himself was not opening up to the spirits. On one or two occasions I noticed that faces were on the point of materialising, but nothing definite appeared.

However, after we had been sitting for about two and a half hours things did start to happen and occurred very quickly. I felt a sudden build up of power and spirits started appearing. I saw my grandfather and then Zeus's face. This aspect of Zeus was different from what I'd seen previously. I wouldn't say it was harsher, but it was more serious. At the time I couldn't make out why or what the difference meant. I wasn't sure it signalled anything, but I feel in the light of what happened that it was trying to convey to me that what I was doing was not meant as entertainment. That there was a serious side to my being here which I shouldn't forget.

I was watching Ray's face, concentrating as I usually do. I felt that it was difficult to keep my eyes open as Ray kept closing his as if in deep thought. However, I kept my eyes open most of the time as I like to watch what happens. I don't suppose I (or anyone) could be prepared for what happened next. I felt my body start to vibrate internally. It was as if everything inside me was swirling around. I had felt vibrations on other occasions, but this was immensely more powerful than anything I had experienced. I had always felt in the past that I could at any time break off if I did not like the experience. This time I felt that I was in a grip of an awesome force. It had such power that I felt I could literally explode as I was under such pressure internally. I am not ashamed to admit that I was unnerved by the experience, but at the same time curious about what was going on. As it happened I was completely in control of my mental faculties and aware of what was taking place around me.

I don't know how long this experience lasted, but it felt like a long time! It appeared to build up and then rapidly subside as Ray started to break off contact with the spirit world. Although I sensed the spirit had left me the effect remained and I felt that my whole being was still in a state of vibration. It was like the aftermath of an electric shock. I remained like this for some hours right through till the following day. I can see why it takes a particular ability to be a physical medium. According to Ray what had occurred had resulted from the build up of anti-matter. Whether or not that was the explanation it was certainly very powerful.

SEANCE WEDNESDAY 13th NOVEMBER 1996

In recent weeks I have not been going to Ray's in the expectation that the phenomena are going to take place. However, things did happen. In one sense it was like going back several months. A whole host of faces appeared rapidly, one after the other. I saw an alien face, then Zeus, followed by that of my grandfather. The spirit world seemed to be saying that all these were linked in some way.

The faces are getting much firmer in appearance. In the past, from the time when I first came to Ray's the spirit faces were ectoplasmic in nature. They looked like descriptions one might read from classic nineteenth century psychic investigations. That appearance has changed dramatically. Now it is almost as if these heads are projecting, three dimensionally, out of Ray's head. They look absolutely solid. It is almost as if you are looking at living, solid flesh. In the past they looked like images or pictures.

Everything that is happening is getting stronger and I wonder where it will all end. Nowadays, when the phenomena occurs in absolutely clear light, as bright as any living room, I see the spirit faces better than when the light is dimmed. (Even when the light is dimmed, there is still plenty of light and I am sitting only a few feet from Ray.) The power in the room seemed so intense that I wasn't surprised when I felt someone settling down on me. It is difficult to describe this sensation. It feels as if your whole body and internal organs are vibrating and changing, but you have no control over it. During this time the whole room was dissolving in colour. It was agitated and bright. It's like sitting in the middle of a coal fire. Yet everything about you is very, very calm.

I felt that we had gone through to another dimension or were just on the verge of going through, but that Ray had stopped at this point. When he stopped everything stopped although I got the impression that spirits were still trying to come through or that other dimensions were still beckoning Ray. I also thought that Ray himself was surprised by the strength of the phenomena. I had felt the power very, very strongly and was agitated for hours afterwards right through to the next day. At lunchtime it seemed suddenly to lift, just in an instant. I felt a bit down as if something was hanging over me and then it just seemed to go.

SEANCE WEDNESDAY 20th NOVEMBER 1996

I arrived at Ray's house at about 8.20pm and sat chatting with him till about 9pm when the phenomena started. Nine o' clock is the time when events often start to happen. When I first came to Ray's, it was this time of the evening that I always associated with the appearance of the spirits.

A series of faces appeared. They materialised in the usual way in that the area around Ray's head seemed to shimmer and move and then the spirits come through. The faces were mainly those I had seen before though, as I recounted in an earlier report, for some weeks the 'familiar' faces did not turn up, but started reappearing recently. The spirit face that looks like me arrived, my grandfather, the chubby-faced individual (the 'joker'). All of those faces appeared in full light even as Ray was talking to me. He remains completely in charge of his faculties while all of this is happening.

The area around Ray was dissolving with greater intensity and a definite alien face appeared. It was thick skinned and the skin looked grey/yellow in colour although this may be simply a distortion produced by the way the phenomena works or my ability to see it. The alien turned into an ape face. It was beautifully clear and the smooth black hair looked so real that you felt you could have reached out and touched it. At the same time I sensed open space and freedom. The ape was very friendly looking almost as if he was pleased to see you and curious about what we were doing.

There was a break and Ray turned down the lights though it was in no sense dark. I could still see Ray quite clearly. About 9.50 pm things started happening again. This time the phenomena seemed even more powerful than before. Several incredible alien faces came through, one after the other. Some looked very unusual, even bizarre to our human eyes. (How do we look to them?) They gave the impression of supreme intelligence. They knew a lot and I was not of any consequence to them. Still, they had made the effort to appear and that must mean something. When the phenomena started to fade (which it does within seconds) Ray muttered some definite, but unintelligible words which sounded as if they were in a strange language.

During the appearance of the phenomena Ray's head appeared to sink into his shoulders and at times it appeared as if something was projecting out of his neck and chin area. His hands were glowing. To me it appeared the room had dissolved and that we had moved beyond this world into another dimension, but not as clearly as I had experienced a few weeks earlier. Around myself I saw glowing areas at my knees and hands. Ray's whole appearance had changed and he looked sunken. There was one alien face that particularly struck me. It was broad faced and looked quite disinterested in our proceedings. The eye sockets were large and projecting. Ray's arms were extended outwards when the alien face appeared. I felt a real aura of strength at this stage as if we were building up to a powerful event. However, Ray stopped things developing and the room was back to normal in an instant.

SEANCE WEDNESDAY 4th DECEMBER 1996

The power came in suddenly at about 8.45pm after we had been sitting chatting for about 40 minutes. A whole variety of spirit faces appeared. At the same time Ray was talking to me - the messages, apparently, were comments made from spirit through him. One comment was that I should be careful about publicity and that I was fooling no one but myself.

Zeus' face materialised repeatedly. This time as an old

man with very prominent eyebrows and golden hair. The face looked so real that I felt as if I could reach out and touch it and that if I had done so I would have felt solid flesh. I was then taken aback by the glimpse of a face with an Adolf Hitler style moustache. I didn't sense at all that this was the man himself. As Ray pointed out such moustaches were common at one time. The only other person I could immediately associate with that style of moustache was Charlie Chaplin. The appearance did confuse me a bit although I suspect that it will become clearer in due course. I also saw a variety of alien faces. This set of events lasted for about ten minutes (from 8.45pm to 8.55pm)

All around me, in bright light, the room was dissolving with an intensity that seemed stronger than usual. I felt the atmosphere pressing hard against my chest. However, as soon as Ray 'resurfaced' the room returned to normal. Ray made a telling comment, 'Without the philosophy or knowledge about the phenomenon, it will not work.' You have to know how it works for it to happen. We had a break for a while then Ray was ready to resume contact with the spirits and turned the lights down. This is easier on the eyes, but doesn't mean that you see the phenomena more clearly. The power now began to build up rapidly. Ray was talking to me all the while about the philosophy and my role in it. 'It's better to be a player in a vast pond then the king of a minute kingdom.'

Faces did appear, but I suspected I was being directed to listen to Ray's words rather than see spirit. The power of the phenomena was immense. The room dissolved into inky blackness and then became a kind of deep coal-red colour (like coal burning in a grate). Ray virtually disappeared. At the same time I could feel the spirits pressing into my chest and see spirit faces covering Ray's head like a silver balloon. He took deep breaths and this seemed to be building up the power of spirit in a controlled way. I felt movement round my face, throat and mouth. I sensed again that somebody was trying to speak through me. Ray's hands were glowing and I could see glowing around my own body.

SEANCE WEDNESDAY 15th JANUARY 1997

At first I thought that there might be no appearance of the phenomena this evening. However, events began to develop rapidly. First of all I saw the grey-haired person who looks like me and who I have seen many times. This time, however, he looked almost as if he was alive in the room ('in the flesh', as I noted at the time). I had never seen him so clearly before. Behind the chair slightly to the right of Ray as I was facing him (that is, to my right) there was an outline of what appeared to be the shape of a human figure, but because it was no higher than the armchair it might have been an aura around Ray.

Then Zeus appeared. I have seen him many times before, but this time it was so much more real. He looked as if he was in the room with us - 'in the flesh' again. There was a definite difference from previous visits because this time Ray's features had changed and had become the actual face of Zeus. The flattened, golden hair on Zeus' forehead was quite clear and prominent. Zeus looked directly at me and gave the impression of being fully alive, just like any person. I was dumbfounded. He looked a bit older than I have seen him before, but this was, perhaps, simply because I could see him more clearly. This face was very different from the ectoplasmic type which tend to be less fleshy looking and often a kind of soup green colour.

All the time that this was taking place, Ray seemed to be engaged in conversation with the spirits. He added that there were several aliens around as he could tell the difference. I asked Ray if he knew that Zeus was there. He said he could feel the 'cobwebs' on his face. I should add that all this took place in bright light with all the usual phenomena - the room dissolving etc. Ray was taking deep breaths and closing his eyes. As he was doing this I felt my

63

own eyes closing and a spirit descend on me. This spirit seemed very powerful. I thought my body was going to explode and had to fight the wish to jump out of the chair! It was as if very powerful vibrations were running through my body and legs. However, I kept looking at Ray and gradually my body seemed to adjust. Once Ray broke contact with spirit the feeling went away, but the after-effects were there for quite a while. Ray then turned the lights down and more faces appeared including that of my grandfather aged about 50-60.

Ray commented that the human race is not significantly advanced in comparison to races (or species) from other worlds and dimensions. As he says we are still at the nursery stage of evolution but our ego refuses to believe it. Then Ray stretched out his arms and the room started to dissolve and move about, making me feel queasy. Again I felt dozy and could not keep my eyes open. I closed my eyes and I could feel someone beside me. My body was vibrating again, but after a while it passed.

SEANCE THURSDAY 23 JANUARY 1997
It was about 10pm when the phenomena started to appear. I'd been sitting with Ray for quite a while chatting. However, I think that what we talked about struck me as important as what we had witnessed. I think that it is true that what I have been neglecting is the philosophy behind what has been taking place. For example, one thing that has been frequently remarked on is the ability of UFOs to appear and disappear in an instant. Clearly, this must mean that 'aliens' are able to move in and out of our dimension at will. Ray has mentioned this to me on several occasions. However, he also pointed out the fact of 'colour vibrations' as discussed by his friend [name deleted] in his manuscript*. I mention this as one aspect of many things that Ray talks about both in and out of contact with the spirits.

As I am writing this I find my mind drawn to the

philosophy rather than to the phenomena I witnessed. This has happened on previous occasions. Ray criticised organised religion, particularly the religious 'professionals' for misleading people. He criticised churches for their wealth and corruption. He pointed to wars and killings carried out in the name of religion especially Christianity and Islam. He also drew attention to the pollution and destruction of the planet by Man. He made the point that if people were made aware of the Earth's place in the wider scheme of things, that is as an insignificant planet, this would cause people to have a fundamental rethink about the way they behave. If people were convinced that there were 'other beings' ('aliens') then it would mean the end of organised religion. People would 'come to their senses.'

Ray often remarks that 'professionals' like scientists think they know everything just because they are experts in their own field. But he made the point that nobody knows everything. There is very little humility shown by the 'eggheads' who would shoot something down just because they believe it can't happen. Ray is often doubtful about the use of trying to convince people when they have this attitude though he would like to show them what can take place - in his own sitting room! He thinks that it is possible to persuade a broader public not by demonstrating his ability, but, perhaps, through convincing an influential person whose word would be listened to. He does want to make the world a better place and, I think, if people realised what a big pool we are REALLY in then it is possible it would make people take a look at themselves and how they behave.

However, the most fascinating aspect I find is the link between the UFO phenomenon and Ancient Egypt. Ray believes he has these links in his life which it would take a book to spell out. However, one key piece of advice that Ray often makes is that to find out what is going on in the present (re UFOs) we must look to the past. He means here (I think) the knowledge of Ancient Egypt and the great spurt of technological advance that took place during that period, for example, the construction of the pyramids (a feat which even modern technology would struggle to carry out). What was the source of these advances? Alien technology seems to be one answer. As Ray points out: if man has been on the Earth for millennia why is it only in the past few hundred years that we have come on leaps and bounds. Ray points to the film 'Stargate' which seems (unintentionally?) to have given an answer. The mechanism in 'Stargate' by which the aliens come through is very similar to the one I have experienced at Ray's. We agreed in future that I would tape Ray's comments in order that these could be fully recorded. [Author's note: We never did!]

*I cannot now recall the significance of this, unfortunately.

SEANCE WEDNESDAY 12th FEBRUARY 1997

Before the phenomenon starts to happen, Ray and I usually spend some time talking. On this occasion Ray talked about how people are sometimes drawn to him because of the spiritual phenomenon without being aware of it themselves. He told me of a girl who came to him for a job even though she later admitted she had no real interest in it and wasn't sure why she had come. As Ray explained, unconsciously, 'she was really there for a different reason', that is to experience or to be made aware of the phenomena.

I should add here that Ray is talking almost as if the influence of the spirits is building up rather like a generator gradually gaining more power. As the spiritual power increases it seems to affect Ray's train of thought so that he loses the sense of what he is thinking and has to stop and recollect what he has been talking about. During the period before the phenomenon occurs Ray asks me questions and I chat to him as if we were simply having a social evening. I told him about the experience of one UFO witness who had felt what he described as 'vibrations inside him' which, in fact, is very much what you feel when the spirit phenomenon occurs. I should mention that Ray had received today some new furniture which we sat in, facing each other. However, this made no difference whatsoever to the appearance of the phenomena.

The phenomenon is subtly different on each occasion. This time as a spirit face started to appear I noticed bright flares of light to my left. The colours that appear vary. This time they were a kind of dark purple. I also saw some beautiful flashes of gold. The room seems to sway from side to side, but I can't say this happens at a specific point in the appearance of the phenomenon. Ray himself seems to physically shrink at times as if he is becoming a different person. His face takes on the shape of another's - well formed rather than the ectoplasm types which I first saw. I noticed this phenomenon starting a few weeks earlier, but it is becoming more pronounced even under bright light. The Greek Zeus-like face looks completely alive.

I would say that (so far) this has not happened to the alien faces. I saw several on this occasion, two in particular which struck me. One had very baggy skin and was broad faced with a wide nose. It looked vaguely human. The second had much tighter facial skin, slightly ruffled, but looked reptilian. It had very sharp features (cheek bones, nose) with slit like eyes.

The power was very strong and at times Ray shuddered and took deep breaths as if trying to control the passage of spirits. Ray explained that he had suffered a bad chest cold, but this did not seem to affect the appearance of the phenomena. I have often wondered whether Ray is aware of the spirits who are passing through. I told him that I had seen my grandfather and he confirmed that he had been aware of his presence. Ray said that he "was just waiting to see if I was going to" say that I had seen him. Ray waits until the person watching says what they have seen as this is confirmation to him about what he has experienced.

SEANCE SUNDAY 23rd MARCH 1997

On this occasion the atmosphere was so strong it was pressing hard against me. It was almost like a physical presence on my stomach which had the effect of making me feel sick. At one point I felt as if I was being gripped by a vice, so strong was the pressure. At this point I did say to Ray that I didn't know how he could stand the physical effects as they must be so enormous on his body. He replied that it was better just to 'go with the flow' and that he didn't feel queasy or suffer any other unpleasant effects from the surge of power. He just felt different. The strength of this feeling was replicated by the number of spirit faces that appeared. It was as if they were all struggling to get in. There was no particular spirit face which seemed to dominate. The Zeus face appeared, flesh like, then merged into the face of another spirit although I didn't recognise the latter one.

The room was shimmering and behind Ray there was a light glow like an aura around his shoulders and head. I could feel a light tickling sensation on my face as if I was being brushed by cobwebs. I have sometimes seen Ray brush his hand across his face as if he too on occasion has this sensation. Ray explained that he was channelling the power and directing it over to me by raising his hands with the palms out as I sit facing him. Ray added that when he spreads his arms outwards he is, as he puts it, 'opening the door' and acting as a channel for the spirit power. Ray did this to demonstrate and I can confirm that when he did this only a few feet away from me in good light, spirit faces appeared. During all this time he was continuing to speak to me and more faces appeared, including Zeus. The room itself turned bright white. At times it was hard to tell if Ray was speaking or someone else was speaking through him. Full light was on the whole time and there was no music. (There is usually a tape playing with a sound similar to running water.)

Ray made one particularly interesting comment: 'the aliens were made to suit the planet, not the planet to suit the aliens.' So who are the aliens? In a sense we are aliens too. I felt that the presence of the spirits was very strong. I said to Ray that I felt it was too strong and because of that there was a kind of block. It was like a rush of water trying to squeeze itself through a narrow channel. I expected a lot more could have happened, but there was something preventing it.

SEANCE WEDNESDAY 26th MARCH 1997

Recently I have felt that things have been quieter at Ray's, as if the spirits have been giving me time to reflect. It has been a lot to take in over the last couple of years. However, two amazing incidents occurred almost out of the blue. I had been sitting for some time chatting to Ray and, in fact, was thinking it was time to leave when suddenly spirit faces started to appear. They came through in quick succession which, I have felt rightly or wrongly, is an indication of how closely these spirits are linked. Or at least that is what they want me to be aware of. One or two faces that I had seen before had passed quickly and then something strange happened. It was as if Ray's face had turned into a statue of gold. A face of shining gold, very thin, projected outwards by several inches. It was a delicate face, but slender as if it had been compressed by pressure on both sides. It looked like the faces you sometimes see in cartoons which have been squeezed into an impossible aquiline shape. It struck me as the face of an ancient Greek God. It looked, I should make clear, absolutely solid. Then two other faces appeared, but, unfortunately, I can't remember the exact sequence.

I think the face that came first was that of Jesus which sounds hard to believe, but that is the thought that flashed into my mind. It looked like the typical European portrayal of Jesus with a pale face, thin nose and features looking peaceful and friendly. I sensed a crown on his head, possibly of thorns. It happened so quickly that it was impossible to be sure, but there was definitely some type of crown there. All around Jesus was a glow which seemed to say that here was a good person. Immediately afterwards the face of Zeus appeared almost as if one had merged into the other. A connection of sorts was quite clearly being indicated.

As if that wasn't enough, as I was about to go Ray reminded me that I had brought my dowsing rods. I took them out and they started to cross at certain points in the room, but centering on where Ray was sitting. I tested this several times to be sure. Ray then came over to see if he could affect the movement of the rods. He stood close by, his hands just outside the rods and said some words to himself over and over again. As he moved his hands round the rods (but NOT touching them) the rods started to move. Where they had been closed they started to open. They opened full out. Ray then carried out the same action and they started to close. What particularly struck me was the effect on my hands. As Ray was influencing the rods I could feel a strange sensation in my arms. The left arm at the wrist and about three inches from there up my lower arms was experiencing a very strong tingling sensation as if there was a direct effect on this part of my arm. The action that the dowsing rods take is really the result of a force running through the body and I was experiencing direct proof that Ray had the ability to interfere with this force and stop it working on the rods. In fact, reversing it. Even stranger was that my right hand was clamped shut. I could not open it and was wondering to myself, 'What the hell's happened!' When Ray moved back things returned to normal again.

It was solid proof to me that the incident at Rosslyn chapel where Ray first affected the operation of the dowsing rods was not a one-off affair. This is testable proof that he can do this whenever he wants to. I don't think that even the scientists will be able to argue against this fact as it can be demonstrated at any time.

CHAPTER FOUR

CONCLUSION: WE ARE NOT ALONE?

That was the last séance I experienced with Ray. I never returned to his flat after 26th March 1997 and broke off all contact with him. That may strike the reader as odd. After all we had been through some incredible experiences which might have led to who knows where? On the other hand, perhaps we had reached the limit of what I was going to see. I can't be sure. What the details of the seances don't reveal was the tension building between us. Ray to my mind was making some ridiculous demands, completely unrelated to the seances, which I found intrusive and out of character. In retrospect, I do believe that the extensive and deep contact he experienced with the spirits affected his personality. Ray wrote to me three times, suggesting we resume the seances and criticising me for abandoning him, as he saw it, but I felt that the relationship between us could never be on the same level of trust. There was maybe fault on both sides.

So what to make of the seances? I stand by what I saw, but what did I in reality see? Spirits of the dead? Phantoms of the mind? No, I'm convinced that it was all part of a reality, but of what I'm not sure. Which brings me to the enigma of it all. Why did these particular spirits or spirit faces appear? Only one consistently materialised that I had a connection with and that was my grandfather - my father's dad. Messages that I've received through other mediums support the idea that he endeavours from beyond the grave to keep in touch. That to me seems a bit odd as he didn't apparently have any particular interest in the spirit world compared with my maternal grandmother who was a medium, but who did not, as far as I was aware, materialise at any of Ray's seances.

So whereas my grandmother didn't appear Zeus did and repeatedly. Why? I'm equally puzzled by the arrival of Peter Cook (died 9th January 1995), Peter Sellers (died 24th July 1980) and Winston Churchill (died 24th January 1965). I had no affinity with any of them and they had no influence on my life - I knew them only by repute. Which must lead to the conclusion that the materialisations may have been symbolic. If that was the case I'm unsure as to what that might be. I knew little of the mythology of ancient Greece compared with ancient Egypt. I had considerably more interest in the latter. Furthermore, there are so many myths and so much symbolism connected to Zeus that it is difficult to discern what might have been significant for my own instruction. There has been the suggestion that in Egypt's Ptolemaic period, Cleopatra being the best know ruler of that era, Zeus, adopted by the Romans, became linked with the god Amen. However, apart from the Egyptian god Bastet appearing in her traditional form as a cat, I wasn't aware of regularly seeing other figures from this highly influential Nile civilisation. So was the overall flow intended to make me aware that the answer to profound questions of life and death lay in the ancient past, as Ray believed?

It is curious, but true that most of the spirit faces I witnessed I did not recognise, neither as well known individuals from history nor deceased friends or relatives. And yet many that materialised looked real and detailed. So why had they arrived? Did they know Ray? Perhaps, but he never suggested that he was familiar with them apart from on the odd occasion - so another puzzle. Over the years that have elapsed since I attended these seances, a significant number of my relatives and acquaintances have 'passed over'. So, perhaps, if the seances were re-run I'd see significantly more recognisable faces. However, what I took out of this experience was a key theme. That there exists other worlds. That there are 'aliens' and they, like humanity, have spirits. We are not alone and are a small part of 'something' unbelievably complex and difficult to comprehend.

APPENDIX I

This document was signed 'Ray' and dated 'August 1986'. I've no idea for whom or what it was written. This was given to me by Ray but I can't recall when. It was headed, 'GUIDELINES'.

1) Check everything twice (at least).

2) Beware concidents [sic: 'coincidence' maybe?] Trust your instincts. Do not believe just because you want to believe.

3) Your motives must always be <u>just</u> and never for selfish reasons.

4) Remember like attracts like. If your thoughts are bad or selfish then that is what you will attract.

5) Never forget there are good and bad spirits. (Forces)

6) Remember that nobody is perfect or knows all on this planet<u>. If they did they would not be here.</u>

7) Beware false friends. Once you attain certain knowledge you will find some people will resent you even though they will not themselves know why. This includes relatives.

8) Never divulge certain knowledge unless asked and the person is worthy of it.

9) You should treat all spirits as you would any stranger until you have checked them out.

10) Never abuse your powers. They can be taken away.

11) Never 'sit' while <u>under the influence </u>of drink or drugs. You may not be in control and attract the wrong forces.

12) Ego is your enemy. It is easy to feel superior to your fellow men and friends.

13) The more you learn the less you will feel you know. For every door you open you will find another behind it.

14) Humility is your friend.

<u>IF YOU READ THIS THREE TIMES YOU WILL NEVER FORGET IT.*</u>

* The whole document was written in upper case, but I felt it was unnecessary to reproduce it in that format.

APPENDIX II

Bob Dean was a well known ufologist and an active speaker at many events. He visited Scotland as part of a tour organised by the US based organisation,' Beyond Boundaries'. I accompanied and assisted the group visiting various sites including Loch Morar, location of the loch 'monster', Morag. Less well known than the inhabitant of Loch Ness, but witnessed many times. One evening I took Bob Dean to visit Ray Tod. Ray was keen that he come and see a demonstration of his mediumship. Unfortunately, for whatever reason, the spirits were reluctant to appear. I myself witnessed several faces though less than usual, but Bob who was admittedly tired after a full day, failed to experience any phenomena. Ray was utterly puzzled and discomfited. I was perplexed. Had the spirits been determined not to appear? That was the conclusion I came to. Bob thanked me for going the extra mile! What I needed was my bed!

ACKNOWLEDGEMENTS

First and foremost my thanks go to my wife Evelyn for reading over the material that made up this book and contributing comments and suggestions which immeasurably improved the end result. This book is dedicated to the memory of my late sister, Morag. I have met and discussed the paranormal with countless people over the past forty years who have all, in various ways, contributed to my continued fascination with the mysteries of the universe and those strange worlds beyond. The mediums Ian Shanes and Katrina McNab were particularly helpful, not to mention my ever enthusiastic colleague and researcher Malcolm Robinson, and fellow organiser of the annual 'UFO and Paranormal' conference Alyson Dunlop.

About the Author
Ron Halliday is a graduate of Edinburgh and Stirling universities. He has been investigating the paranormal for over 40 years and was founder and chairman of the investigative group, 'Scottish Earth Mysteries Research'. He has written several books and contributed to many television and radio programmes including BBC's 'Newsnight'. For a number of years he wrote the 'X-Files' column for the Glasgow 'Evening Times'. Ron's publications include:
'UFOs: the Scottish Dimension', 'Scottish Paranormal Press', 1997.
'McX: Scotland's X Files', editor and contributor, B&W Publishing, 1997.
'UFO Scotland', B&W Publishing, 1998.
'The A-Z of Paranormal Scotland', B&W Publishing, 2000.
'Evil Scotland', Fort Publishing, 2003.
'Haunted Glasgow', Fort Publishing, 2008.
'Edinburgh After Dark', B&W Publishing, 2010.
'Famous Scots and the Supernatural', B&W Publishing, 2012.

'Mysteries of the Scottish Landscape', Aura publications, 1988

Note that 'Phenomenal News' the publication of 'Scottish Earth Mysteries Research' contains articles on Ray Tod.

The author can be contacted via 'Facebook' or by emailing ronhalliday168@sky.com

Printed in Great Britain
by Amazon